1

CHARMED
From Motown to Combat and Back!

A Memoir

By
Tom McAuliffe

NEXT STOP PARADISE PUBLISHING
Ft. Walton Beach, Florida, USA

Charmed
From Motown to Combat and Back

by Tom McAuliffe

100% of the profits of this book will be donated to
NORMAL
The National Association for the Reform of Marijuana Laws

First Edition - 2023

For more information email:
bookinfo@nextstopparadise.com

WWW.AUTHORTOMMCAULIFFE.COM

DEDICATIONS

For my Wife, my Love and my Life, Sharon

For those who have helped me along the way
or at least didn't call the Cops!

And for anyone who has ever been told they should
'just give up!'

On the Cover:

(Left): 16mm Film shoot in the Bahamas
        Cruise Ship Duo with 'Luki'
        High School Band with Grack and Jerry
        Las Vegas Performer at various clubs
(Right): Las Vegas Singing Comedian, The Flamingo
        Motown Revu, Fox Theater, Detroit
        SS Vanguard Cruise Ship
        PH2-AC Tom McAuliffe, USN

☻ TABLE OF CONTENTS ☻

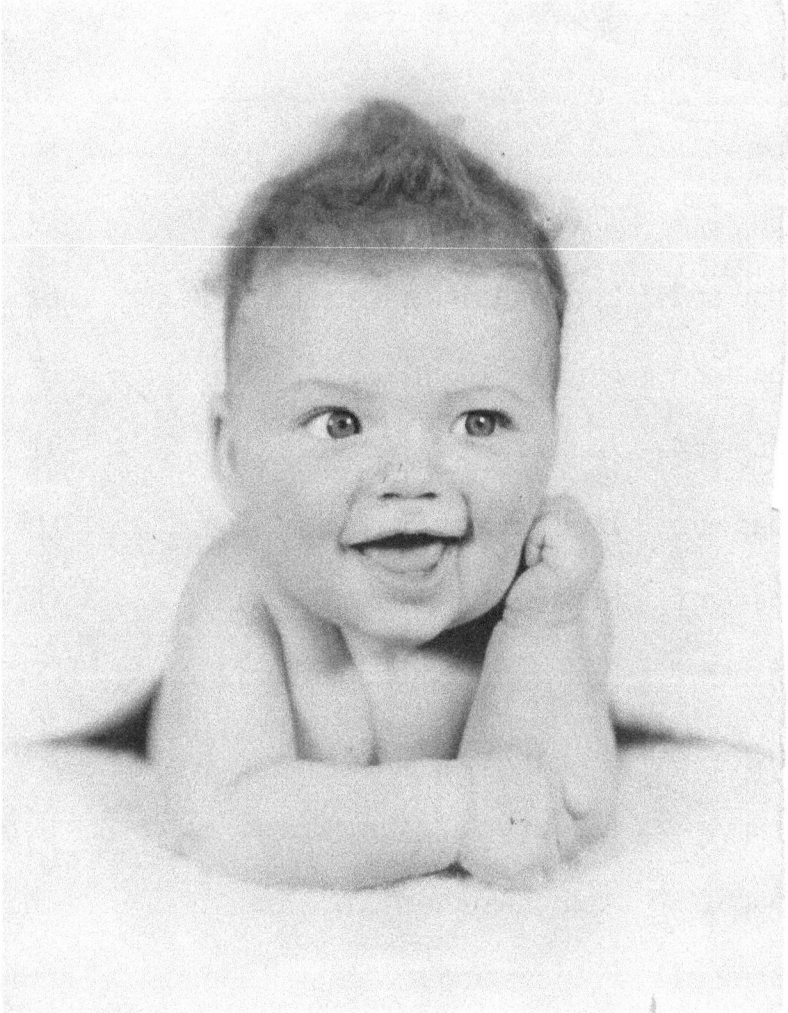

Thomas Patrick McAuliffe

PREFACE

Writing about oneself is perhaps the pinnacle of narcissism, but when you've lived a life that's engaging, intriguing, and full of captivating stories that others might find edifying, it's necessary. I grew up on the Northwest side of Detroit as the youngest son of an alcoholic city firefighter and a stay-at-home mother, which led me to believe that I was, all things considered, a very typical individual. I have truly been blessed, and I feel as though I've lived a privileged life to the point where I've nearly been able to emulate Forrest Gump in my capacity to be on the periphery of big events and renowned individuals. I have indeed been fortunate.

It seems that luck has always been on my side. The phrase "The kid could fall in a bucket of shit and come out smellin' like a rose!" was a common one used by my Mom. For instance, I enlist in the United States Navy and despite the fact that there were no assurances and I could have wound up chipping paint for four years, I was selected for the Naval Schools of Photography. Exactly what I wanted. Maybe I should have a career in politics? I end up working for a key Representative at the state legislature. I step up to a microphone, start singing, and then the next thing I know, I'm working as a performer in Las Vegas and on cruise ships. Indeed, I've been afforded many opportunities. And this is not to suggest that there haven't been a lot of obstacles along the way; from the fact that my father was an alcoholic firefighter to suffering with addictions and Attention Deficit

Hyperactivity Disorder (ADHD) and Post Traumatic Stress Disorder (PTSD). My family is also dysfunctional and estranged. I miss them. Lesson 1? Value family.

Now, I'd want to tell you that I'm a man who has made his own way in the world and much of what I have today is the result of my own relentless hard work, and that's mostly true… I've never received anything from anyone, but at the same time, I've been fortunate to have people who believed in me, recognized my talents, and gave me opportunities to prove myself. So, when politicians claim that personal success is not solely an individual effort, they're correct in the sense that we don't exist in a vacuum. We rely on each other for encouragement, support, and guidance.

I've been exceptionally lucky to have the opportunity to learn from wise advisors along the way.

I've never held a 9 to 5. Ever. The closest I came was when I served as the Director of Public Relations for a prominent Silicon Valley media company. My natural inclination has always been toward entrepreneurship. The digital media

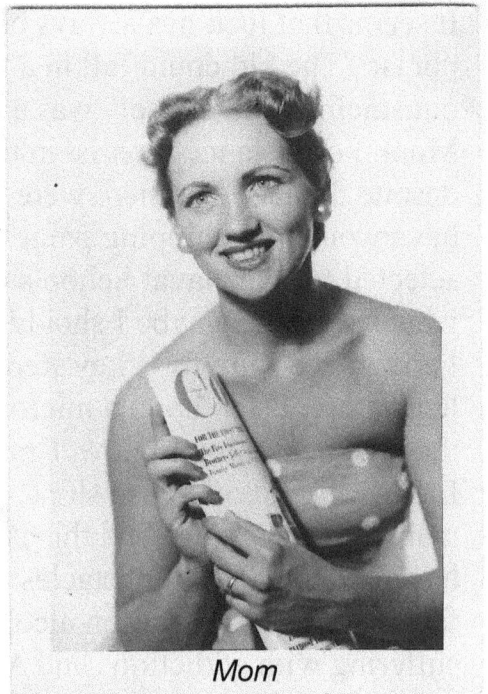

Mom

revolution, in which I played a small part, led me to believe that investing over a million dollars in a college degree is often a misguided endeavor. The Internet streaming revolution has transformed the media and learning landscape entirely.

In the following pages, I'll most likely make a great number of errors, and I hope that those who are mentioned (or not mentioned) will forgive me. I have made every effort to remember details correctly. As the lyrics of the song go, "What a long strange trip it's been." My life, much like anyone's, has been marked by moments of sadness and sorrow, but more often than not, it has been filled with joy and laughter. After 60 plus years, it's nearly impossible to remember every conversation, but I'm blessed with a robust memory and have kept copious notes. There are some things that stick out in my memory, and I will try to share them with you here for your edification rather than for the sake of my own ego. Everyone has a responsibility to look for the good in bad situations. Hone the ability to laugh in the face of adversity. It's a tonic!

And now that we've gotten that out of the way... I don't mean to brag, but seriously, can you think of anyone else who has; flown in the F-14 Tomcat Fighter Jet, bombed as a Comedian in front of 300 people in Las Vegas, earned the title 'King of San Francisco Karaoke' according to SF Weekly Magazine, released three music CDs (none of which are worth a damn yet sold thousands), authored numerous books that are worth a damn, gigged in places that should have been condemned while touring from Hawaii to New York, Europe to Florida, someone who became a Journeyman in Commercial Photography and has been a royal pain in the rear end ever since he first learned how to walk? And if you do know someone who fits that description, could you please have him give me a call? I really hope that my words might provide you with some motivation, since if I can triumph over adversity with humor and dogged determination, then anyone can.

I grew up in a neighborhood near Redford on the Northwest side of Detroit. There, I had a very typical middle-class Norman Rockwell like upbringing. My childhood home was on a street that was flanked with enormous Dutch elm trees, which created a sort of picturesque tunnel. During the warmer months, a shade tunnel; during the colder months, a snow tunnel. It was remarkable… at least in my eyes. That's how it all seemed to me when I was 8 years old and living on Heyden Street. I was the youngest of four children, and despite being the focus of things most of the time, I was sometimes disregarded because I was the youngest I guess. More on that later…

Mom

My parents did a excellent job of hiding the fact that their marriage was falling apart in the middle of the 1960s, at

Dad

least as far as I could tell being the youngest of four children. Due to the fact that both of my sisters and brother were 10 years older than I was, it was almost as if we were two separate families. Tommy was the lovely little shit who could do no wrong because he was Daddy and Mama's pride and joy. The things that I got away with my brother and sisters never could. Music was always big for me and when things got difficult, I would let the music carry me away so I could escape it all. I would daydream about living a life that was more serene.

Having been in close proximity to historic events on multiple occasions… I'm like the 'Forest Gump' of Detroit rock-n-roll… Moreover, the experiences I had while serving in the United States Navy were one of a kind. I believe that reading all of it will provide you with a unique and intriguing reading experience. I am living proof that someone with a little bit of talent who's willing to use all of it is always going to be further ahead than someone who sits on their behind resting upon previous accomplishments, nice looks, or fortunate circumstances.

For me, it's always been about three things: being prepared, having the balls to believe, and being in the right place at the right moment. My experience has also taught me that other people will believe about you what you believe about you. If you behave like you belong, you actually do belong, and you'll be left alone…every damn time…*if* you act like you belong. But you've got to be ready and you've got to have the skills and talent to back it up you can't be just all talk and no action. I know I've tried and bullshit will only get you so far. Don't look at me like that. Sometimes BS is better than the truth. And I'm not talking about hurtful lies here.

I've made an effort to remember what took place throughout this crazy voyage as accurately as I can. If there's one thing that today's events can teach us, it's that when two individuals look at the same thing, they might walk away with completely different interpretations of what they saw.

From the Rock-n-Roll scene in Detroit and elsewhere to serving in the Combat Camera Group of the United States Navy, to working as a low-level performer in Las Vegas and the Cruise Lines, to now just being a regular stiff just trying to go through life without hurting himself or anyone else… I offer you my best wishes in the hopes that the experiences I've had may be of some use in your own life and that you will find these pages to be both inspirational and entertaining. As the great Jackie Gleason always said… 'And awwwwwwway we go!'

☉

FORWARD

Let's get right down to it… I'd love it if I could have a cool actor or an influential person or a high-profile individual write a cool Forward and include it in this section. The reality is, however, that although I have met a great number of renowned people, the vast majority of them were not really good people and were not individuals whom I would consider to be friends. And that brings me to another point: I don't actually have all that many friends in this day and age. Because of my advanced age, I am quite picky about the people I allow into my life and with whom I choose to have a relationship. It's probably unfortunate, but I've just been burned one too many times. And I'm sure I'm not innocent too.

However, I did have an offer from a state senator in Florida, and the editor of a large magazine, as well as the lead guitarist of a semi-famous band and a very prominent actress from Hollywood, all wanted to try their hand at it. However, I do not require, and you most certainly do not wish to read, a whole bunch of self-congratulatory drivel about what a fantastic man I am and everything that I have achieved or experienced in my life. Who has time for that–what a waste!

Let's do this instead and save some time for the two of us. Kay? I have made an effort to be a good person and to do unto others, and I hope that you've made an effort to do the same. People are only as morally upstanding as

they persuade themselves to be. You want to have a nasty attitude and screw others over… well, guess what? Karma is a real thing, and I've seen many people get what's coming to them (and ironically, those people are always the ones who scream the loudest).

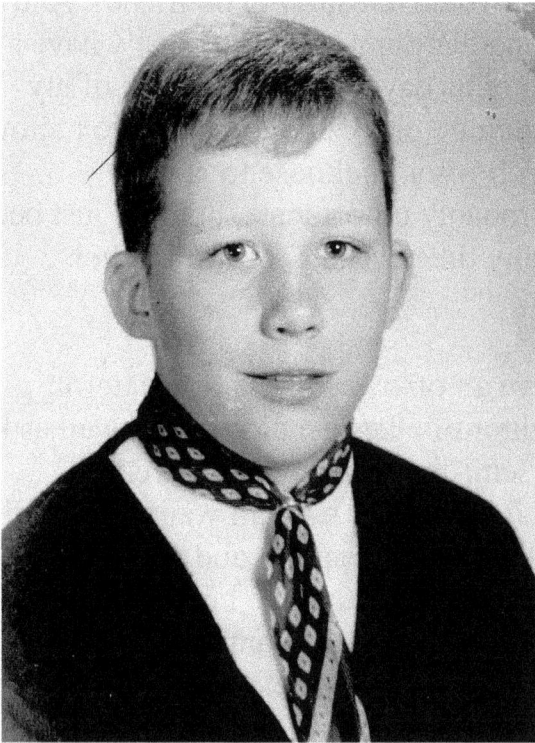

It's true that luck has been on my side. There were numerous instances in which I should not have been successful; as a result of a troubled adolescence that led me down the wrong path. I entered the Navy without any promises, and I talked my way into one of the most wanted

occupations in the fleet: that of a combat photojournalist. I was never afraid to put myself in dangerous situations in order to capture the photo I wanted, whether it was flying in the door of a helicopter doing 200 miles per hour or going 40 feet below the water. In both music and comedy, I have always given 110% of myself to the audience, and I've never been reluctant to make myself the punchline of a joke for the sake of providing them with entertainment… for the laughs. In my written work, I've made it a point to give readers information that's not only accurate but also interesting.

Someone like me, who possesses only a moderate amount of talent, is always going to be further ahead of someone who has a great deal of ability but does nothing with it. I think this is what I am trying to say. To find out what you're capable of in life, you have to test yourself by participating in the real world. Living life on the

couch is not how it was intended to be lived! And the fear
of failing can prevent a person from living a full life
that's rich and rewarding. We need to feel free to fail.

I really do hope that I've been able to save you some
time, and maybe even more than that… I have a sincere
desire that the experiences I share in this book will either
provide you with food for thought or will help make your
life better… at the very least, provide you with some
good laughs. Have fun!

Elaine, Diane, Matt, Tom

CHAPTER 1

The Heyden Hillbillies
Redford in the 60s

"The 'Luck of the Irish' is no luck at all!"
Unknown

My family was Irish Catholic, and we lived in the
Northwest part of Detroit. I attended Christ the King
Catholic school, which is located in Redford on Grand
River Avenue. I must admit, I was quite a handful for the
Sisters, especially when they were clad up in their
traditional Penguin-like 'Habits'. I was a royal pain in the
ass. My size, relative to my age, often made me appear as
if I belonged in a higher grade. In later times, I had the
delusion that I was sitting at my regular desk, but in
reality, I was waiting outside the office of Mother
Superior in those large and uncomfortable wooden chairs.

One of my most ingrained recollections is the occasion
when I was summoned to her office, and after a short
conversation, she just pointed. The 'Board of Education'
was hanging on the wall on the other side of the room
from its enormous brass hook. It was a piece of wood
roughly two feet long, equipped with a handle and clearly
labeled 'Board of Education'. It had strategically placed
holes to minimize air resistance, ensuring the Sister could
deliver a good swing. After I had retrieved the paddle, the
journey back to Sister was a excruciatingly long one.

FEB

20

I remember that one of the things I always had a problem with, in addition to my normal incorrigibility and my sass, was when we had to participate in the civil defense drills. When I just told the sisters that I felt it was silly that we were hiding under desks from a 20-megaton nuclear blast, I was given a hard time for not cooperating, and they took it as a sign that I was being disobedient. Even though I was not the sharpest tool in the box, even I realized that trying to hide under a desk while they were detonating a thermal nuclear weapon would offer very little, if any, protection. Though I was young I was not particularly dim-witted and I felt the whole enterprise was absurd. I made my opinion known. Not good. The good Sisters were intolerant of dissent.

In the city of Detroit, the neighborhood of Redford was a regular community complete with its own library, schools, churches, shopping centers, and more. My favorite Hollywood heroes would always come out on top in the end, and I would spend many happy hours at the Redford Theater watching them. After some time, my mother started letting me walk the considerable distance up to the theater on my own. I distinctly recall watching Elvis and his blue racing car with Ann Margret multiple times in a row. I also enjoyed other classics like The Beatles in 'Help'. The Redford movie theater is still operating to this day, and the hot popcorn with butter is the very best you will ever taste.

My mother was left with four children and absolutely no professional skills after my father left the family around the year 1966. I recall going with her to different job interviews, and eventually, she got a job working in the "secretarial pool" at Honeywell Inc. It was like something out of a movie. She took me to her office on a weekend just so I could see it. Inside this room, which was the size of an acre, were rows upon rows of desks occupied by young ladies who were busily

Diane and Tom

typing away come Monday. In the thirty years that she worked for the company, Mom worked her way up from the secretarial pool to the position of Administrative Assistant to the President of the company. She had every reason to be quite proud of this accomplishment. Pretty damn good for someone who had only a high school education and no experience.

Christ the King Elementary, about ten blocks away from our home on Heyden, is where I have some of my first memories of attending school. The queens of discipline didn't put up with any nonsense. They reigned with an iron fist, which, in my experience, typically took the form of a gigantic ruler. The sisters of perpetual misery were firm believers in the use of physical discipline, and with a child as difficult to control as I was, it was one of the only ways to cut through the noise, grab my attention, and convey the intended lesson. And sometimes that

wasn't enough and only built anger and resentment in me.

There were uniforms for both boys and girls. Girls wore a Navy pleated skirt, white blouse, and a navy blue scarf, while boys wore dark or khaki slacks, light blue shirts, and dark navy blue clip-on ties. Having students wear uniforms, levels the playing field by ensuring that children from all socioeconomic backgrounds have access to the same clothing. Smart.

I was the naughty kid who grew up on the wrong side of the tracks and could never be changed. I remember that when I was in about the third grade, we were instructed to line up along the exterior of this structure, and along that wall, there were small windows that ranged in size from about 11 by 14 inches in a variety of colors.

To this day, I cannot tell you why, but I impulsively decided to punch one of those windows with my fist. I

have no idea why I did it, but I think I did it out of some strange curiosity about what it would be like. I was grounded for three days because my Mom was so upset. I'll never forget the expression of disappointment on my mom's face as she saw me sitting in Mother Superior's office. It didn't leave an imprint that lasted very long, but I remember it as being one of the first times I ever managed to make my mother truly upset.

The penguins had stringent rules, and there were some aspects of their culture that I simply have never been able to comprehend, not even to this day. For instance, I remember when they used to urge girls not to wear shiny patent leather shoes because boys would use the reflection in the shoes to look up their skirts. To a large extent, I found the nuns to be selfless, dedicated educators who sincerely loved children and considered their teaching as a form of service to both people and to God. This is despite the fact that a few of them were just this side of being a pervert and who had no real business being anywhere near children.

After I had been attending Christ the King Elementary for around three semesters, Mother Superior brought my mother in and informed her that they had reached the limit of what they were able to deal with and that they believed my behavior required placement in a more 'comprehensive facility' where I could get 'Help'.

My ADHD and hyperactivity were significant contributors to my incorrigibility. In those days, of course, we had no genuine knowledge regarding matters of Diet and how the use of sugar might alter behavior. These were concepts that were still in their infancy at the time. In retrospect, I can state that one of the reasons I was bouncing off the walls was due to the massive amount of sugar that I was consuming; cakes, pies, cookies, ice cream, and candy were all on the menu at the time. It should not have come as a surprise that I was unable to sit still. Both as a reward system as well as a coping mechanism sugar was there… Are you having a hard time? Have a sundae with some hot fudge! Do you want to celebrate the good score on the test? What about a delicious chocolate bar? My fast energy metabolism and my hyperactivity were the only things that prevented me from reaching a weight of 400 pounds. So as my mother toiled away to keep a roof over our heads and food on the table, I ran the streets.

The people who lived on our street of Heyden were known as 'the Heyden Hillbillies,' why is beyond me. At first, Mom said that everyone must "be home by the time the street lights are on!" Later on, as that was continually disregarded, the rule eventually evolved into "be home

by 11 PM!" Still further on, it eventually evolved into "please call and let me know where you are." My mother, Doris, was always referred to by her first name, and as time went on, she became known as 'Grandma Doe.' For some reason, people never addressed her by her last name. She was not a believer in being a "helicopter parent," and she was of the opinion that her children should have the independence to explore life on their own. As a result, I ran the streets with my buddies, and when we weren't getting into boyish pranks and petty larceny, we learned that there was a fun life downtown in the big lights.

Three important roads—Grande River, Woodward, and Gratiot—lead from Downtown to the suburbs like the spokes of a wheel. Detroit is split by these three big boulevards. When I was around 11 or 12 years old, I realized that we could hop on a bus for approximately one dollar and travel from our quiet, peaceful existence in the suburbs into the commotion and brilliant lights of downtown via the Grand River Express. This was a revelation for me. There were many lovely days that I spent watching baseball at Tiger Stadium. Other afternoons were spent at the historic Fox Theater and for $4.50 watching the Motown Revue with performers like Little Stevie Wonder, Martha Reeves and the Vandellas, and the Four Tops, just to name a few. The Grande Ballroom, The Vanity Ballroom, The Eastown, and later a variety of clubs from Downtown Detroit to Ann Arbor were also some of the settings where I had the good fortune to witness performances by performers who would go on to achieve local and tremendous national success as recording artists. I always found a way in...always.

My buddies were usually annoyed by the fact that they were always 'carded' and had to present their phony IDs, but I was always able to sail through security without any problems. Please keep in mind that I am between 14 and 15 years old, and on many occasions, my friends and I were the only white people present. But that was never an issue for us. When we got into it with some guys from the other side of town, that's when I first became aware of the rivalry that exists between the Eastside and the Westside of town. Otherwise it was always… 'peace, love, and dope!'

Dad & The AA Gene

My father struggled with alcoholism… And he wasn't the kind of drunk who would hurt somebody; he was more of the "lampshade on his head" variety. Along with many of his cousins and in-laws, he worked as a firefighter in Detroit. He put himself in one of the most precarious situations by choosing to drive the hook and ladder fire engine. The long hook and ladder is equipped with a steering position at the back, which enables them to maneuver around turns. Once I asked my Dad why he drank so much, he responded in a pretty cavalier manner saying, "Son, if you drove the back of a Hook and Ladder at 3 AM on Black ice, you'd drink too!" It was remarked in jest, but I think there may have been some truth to it. If he had fear he never showed it.

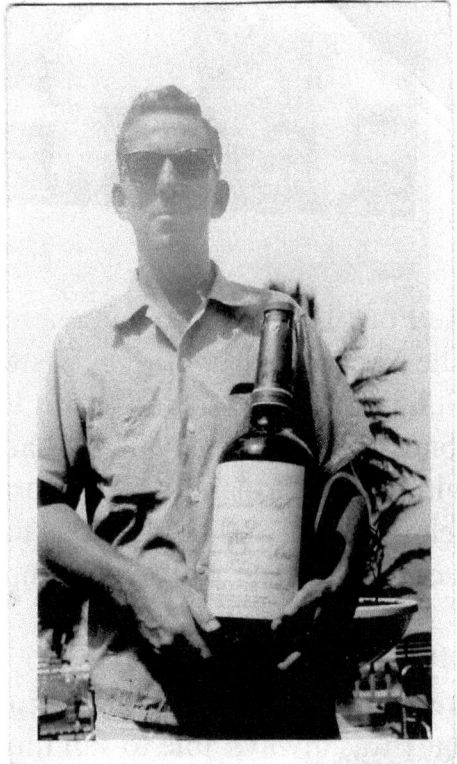

Maybe the booze hid it. One thing is sure… it takes a special man to do his job. Dad, just like his father-in-law, brother-in-law, and cousin before him, served his entire life as a firefighter in Detroit. My recollections of trips to his Firehouse are very clear, and I even got to slide down the pole a few times. These firehouses were built in the traditional style with green walls and black and white tile floors. The firefighters worked shifts of four days on and three days off and slept at the fire station. During the early 1960s, my Grandfather, Alfred Kruck, served as the first Fire Chief of Southfield, a suburb of Detroit. He was also responsible for bringing Paramedics into the city. They considered him to be completely insane at first. Firefighting has always played a significant role in my family. Sometimes when my Dad would come home from fighting a fire, his uniform would smell like burning leaves in the fall. Its funny the things one remembers.

Another perk of having a father who worked as a firefighter in Detroit was that every once in a while, a huge red fire engine would drive up to our house, and all of the kids in the neighborhood would gather outside to look it over. When a firefighter had their hat on, they were considered to be on duty; however, once they removed their hat, they were no longer considered to be on duty and were free to enjoy a beer or two. And I can recall very clearly how, when my father was abstaining from alcohol and working hard to overcome his alcoholism, the guys would come over, and he would get them a beer, but he wouldn't drink any of it himself. I was only about seven years old when this happened, so I didn't fully grasp everything that was going on, but I did understand that my father was attempting to wean himself off of alcohol. I remember that we stored the hard liquor above the icebox. I became concerned when I saw him go to the liquor cabinet, and I meekly questioned him, "Are ya gonna drink today?" and he responded, "Nope, not today." He then proceeded to get the liquor out for his buddies so that they could have a few drinks in the basement. I can't help but think back on how proud I was of him. Unfortunately, in 1973, he passed away from cirrhosis of the liver despite making several attempts to quit drinking and even working through the steps of Alcoholics Anonymous. Sometimes, nothing works. Like any addiction it's unrelenting.

Being the child of an alcoholic presents a number of difficulties, not the least of which, it seems to me, is the alcoholism gene that was passed on to us children. Everyone here has, at some point or another, struggled with substance misuse of some kind, whether it be alcohol, drugs, gambling, sex or even food. Some of us won't confess it publicly or even to ourselves, but we all have. I have come to the conclusion that the human body contains a gene that, when a person has consumed a particular amount of alcohol or a substance, activates a gene that causes them to become addicted to that substance or activity. This might happen at any age, whether the person is 15 or 50 years old. It is possible for it to occur after one or two drinks, but it is also possible for it to occur after 40 years of drinking. I know a 17-year-old guy who drank a few beers and became a drunk, and I know another 17-year-old boy who tooted two lines of Cocaine, and about a week later, I saw him going out of a downtown pawn shop after hocking his Rolex! Although I'm not a medical professional, my observations have led me to this conclusion. Addiction is a freaking monster that is sneaky by its very nature, which makes it much more insidious when it involves things like food or gambling. Throughout my life, not only have I struggled with a drug and sugar addiction, but my siblings have also had challenges, albeit to varying degrees of success and failure. Even now, I have to fight this war daily. Alcoholism is the Irish curse... it's an illness, all right! As I've said, Robert, my Dad, was, at least to all appearances, a merry alcoholic. Knowing what I know now, I can see that one of the primary aspects of his alcoholism, and it's different for every sufferer, was his relationship with his celebrity Father, world-famous champion armless golfer and 'Ripley's Believe It or Not' alumnus Tommy McAuliffe.

Knowing what I know now, I can see that one of the main components of his alcoholism was that he believed he could never live up to the reputation of his world-famous father. And I remember Grandpa riding his son like a jockey in the Kentucky Derby. He felt that his son was destined to fail, and Grandpa Tommy never considered anything to be satisfactory in any way. (I would be grateful if you would take the time to read my book 'Mr. Mulligan: World Famous Champion Armless Golfer Tommy McAuliffe') Even though I was very young at the time, I've a distinct memory of my Grandfather yelling at my Dad while we were sitting in his truck in the driveway. Grandpa was very successful in the insurance industry, and it was decided that my Dad would start a business called "McAuliffe Insurance Repair" to take care of grandpa's customers whenever the need arose. All of this was done not only to generate extra income but also in an effort to win the approval of a father who was incapable of expressing either love or encouragement. When you add to all of that the pressure of the Fire Department and driving the Hook and Ladder, it's little wonder that more problems didn't develop. To set the record straight, however, I don't recall him ever being violent, at least not toward me. By 1964, Doris, my Mom, and the four of us children had all left Dad's life. A little over 5 years later, he passed away in a sanitarium just outside of Detroit from complications related to cirrhosis of the liver.

Some memories are etched in stone. Once I saw my Dad run into a burning house because they thought there were people inside. But 'Bob' wouldn't stop what he was doing and put on his oxygen mask and tank like the other firefighters did. When I was a little, one of my all-time favorite things to do was to dance on top of my father's feet. And as we were doing that one time, I asked him about his lack of oxygen gear at the fire and how his actions terrified me. And we continued to do that for a while. And he explained that the people inside couldn't wait, and that the people inside don't pay him to wear oxygen; rather, they pay him to "eat fire." Stupid...but definitely macho. He was a mystery to unravel. When I got home from school in the third grade with a test that was graded D+, I felt for sure that both my father and my mother would be angry with me. That memory will be with me forever. The response that Dad gave to one of the questions in particular took everyone by surprise. You had to choose a word that corresponded to the statement; for instance, the question read, "I was dancing with my gorgeous A) Partner B) Date C) Wife or D) Target... so I pieced the phrase together to read, "I was dancing with my lovely target," and for some reason, it made my father laugh and laugh. The only thing I can think of is that there were a lot of spy shows like 'Man from Uncle' on television at the time. Who knows, but his reaction was unexpected, and it was the first time I really realized that I could make him laugh. My dad and I used to spend a lot of time together watching television shows like Gunsmoke, The Rifleman, Bonanza, and others while sitting in his overstuffed Burgundy chair. Even though I was very young at the time, I look back on those evenings as lovely and unforgettable. I was taught at a young age the importance of being honest.

Boys Will Be Boys?

Around 1967, when I was ten, they made the discovery that Tom was "out of control," when in reality he was just in need of some strong guidance. I had a general attitude of "fuck you" toward anyone in a position of power and relished challenging the status quo. When trying to correct or reprimand me, most people gave up and just threw up their hands when they realized it wouldn't have any real effect on me. And there was no doubt that I was going in the wrong direction, which meant that I would either end up in a psychiatric hospital, the state penitentiary, or dead. Hawthorne Center, located in Northville, Michigan, is a facility that is known all over the world for the psychiatric treatment of children who are emotionally disturbed. I was to be a client.

I had to travel a long and arduous path before I realized that it was impossible to simply say "fuck you" to everyone and everything and come out of it alive. People will simply withdraw and stop dealing with you, but I did it anyway. During this time, I also appear to have developed a dislike for telling the truth. I discovered that I was saying ridiculous things that I was well aware were not true, and the more ridiculous they were, the better. Part of it may have been psychotic delusion, but part of it was just for fun, just to get a rise out of the other person or to see their eyes become really big. I'm aware that this seems childish, but it's the truth. I was a child at the time. When I was around six or seven years old, one of my favorite television shows was called 'Man from Uncle.' Inspired by this show, I actually concocted a fiction in which I was a covert agent and that my family's backyard included an underground spy base. The establishment? It consisted primarily of a large pit that we had dug, with some plywood boards placed over the top of it. I excavated a hole in the side and placed a dashboard that we had recovered from an old car… N\now, it was a top-secret control center!

During those early years, we also spent a lot of time playing Army, much like the majority of young guys…. The battles we fought were epic, and they began when a few of my friends on the street where I lived met and became aware of a similar group of boys on the street next to us, Kentfield Ave. From that point on, the battles raged. The battles we fought were extremely large, with 10–12 players participating; the game was similar to a version of "Steal the Flag." We would play a game in which we would place an object, such as a boot, a frisbee, or something else, on the roof of our fort and challenge the other boys to steal it. Our weaponry was made of wood either swords or one of the Dads's fashioned machine guns out of wood. One memory I have is being taken prisoner by the opposing side and being held captive in their stronghold. I was literally chained down and tied up. After not finding me for the better part of an afternoon, my mother alerted the search party, which consisted of my brother, who eventually located and freed me. He's my hero!

That describes a lot of what my brother Matt was and still is… if you were in difficulty, you could phone him, and he would come to help you. I will never forget that there was one other Saturday morning when I got up early and walked to the O'Neil's house at the end of the block. It was around eight in the morning. I was just goofing about when I took a tumble, injured my knee, and became unable to walk. My mother found out about it somehow, and roused my brother early on a Saturday morning so that he could carry me back home. He did this while wearing his white boxer shorts from Sears, walking to the end of the street where I was sitting crying on the corner.

As I was growing up, I was never really made aware of our family's financial situation. Regardless of the highs and lows that may have occurred in the McAuliffe household at any one time, my mother would nearly always make sure to provide a delicious meal for all of us on Sundays. We would place it in the dining room, complete with a tablecloth made of cloth, cloth napkins, China, and two forks. Every time, we would invariably have roast beef or something similar, a salad, and fresh buns. She made a point of accomplishing a lot with a little, which helped me understand frugality.

In a later stage of my adolescence, when I was being particularly rebellious, I moved the china cabinet off of its base, tipping it over and thus destroying my mother's collection of china. Although I will carry that remorse with me for the rest of my life, it did teach me an important lesson: there are certain actions that simply can't be undone. I was probably seven or eight years old and a handful with uncontrollable ADHD. Pass the chocolate sauce will ya please?

Hawthorn Center

I was the incorrigible poster child for problematic adolescents, thus I ended up as a patient at the world-famous Hawthorn Center in Northville, Michigan. It was one of the lowest points in my life.

Memories are funny things. My adolescence was tough. The tantrum I threw after learning that my Mom and sister Elaine would not be returning to the center and would be leaving me there instead, was epic. I was led reluctantly to my new room, where I beat on the metal screens that covered all of the windows and watched as they got into Mom's yellow Oldsmobile and simply drove away. Suddenly, a bag appeared with all of my belongings in it. I was told to unpack. Mom and company probably believed they were doing the right thing. As they were leaving me alone with complete strangers for the very first time in my life, I stood at the window

staring out in shock as they drove away. I was exactly eight years old at the time.

First, I was sobbing because my heart was breaking, and I didn't understand how they could do this to me (to this day, I still struggle with abandonment issues), but then I just became angry and started throwing things... Soon after that, two enormous black men in white uniforms and a nurse arrived. In short order, they tossed my ass on the bed and dressed me in a dazzling white jacket with a variety of fantastic buckles. After that, they escorted me to a room that they referred to as the "QR," which stood for "Quite Room." It was a cell that was 15 feet by 20 feet and contained a metal bed, as well as the previously described windows with metal screens. The room was painted in a calming medical green with tiled floors. The cell doors were made of solid oak and measured four inches thick. It also featured a tiny window through which the personnel could check on the 'patient' and observe them. The QR was essentially an empty padded cell without the pads. Shortly after my "outburst," I told them in a straight forward manner that I was not going to do what they wanted and that I was pretty adamant about this. After that, a very tall black man named Charles who was 6 feet 7 inches tall said he begged to differ. He utilized this unique and effective method of correction... He had enormous hands and was able to hold a basketball with only one hand. If he saw you were misbehaving, he would just walk up to you and give you a thump on the head with his middle finger. This was quite effective but is probably illegal now.

You intend to have a temper tantrum? When that happened to me, the two guys dressed in white would lift me up by each arm and carry me down the corridor to the QR. It was exactly like everything you've seen in the movies. You could scream your lungs out for hours, and no one would ever hear you, nor would they give a rat's behind about anything you had to say. To this day, I have a severe aversion to being confined in tight quarters. If you become even more out of control, they had straight jackets that they could put you in. Although I never reached that point again, several of the other patients there did. So there I was, in the hospital's ward, with Dr. Galligan as my attending psychologist. We got to work

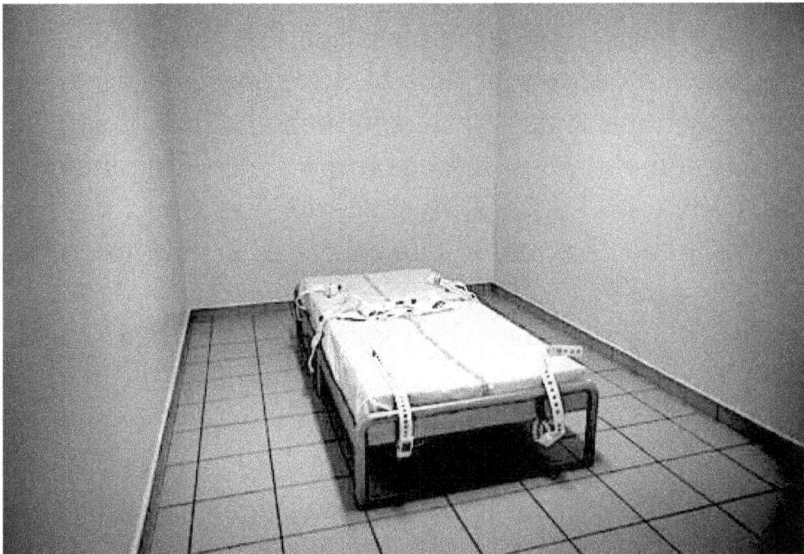

on solving some of Tom's problems, or at the very least, figuring out what those problems might be. I detested it when other people told me what to do. At the same time the simple truth was that I blamed myself for the

dissolution of my family. But the statement that, "Tommy was the reason why Dad left" could not be further from the truth. Nobody bothered to tell *me* that.

In the arrogant years of my youth, Tommy had made it clear that he was going to do whatever the hell he wanted, whenever he wanted, and that the ramifications were irrelevant. As a result, it came as a rude awakening to learn that I was, in fact, helpless and that I would be compelled to obey regardless of the circumstances or my own objections. This was accomplished quite effectively by putting me in a soundproof room and sealing the door behind me until I agreed. At the time, my animosity toward my doctors and my mother was at a boiling point, and I stopped talking to her for at least a couple of months following being dropped off. I saw Doctor Galligan on a almost daily basis for therapy. During those sessions, we would either talk or draw while we talked to each other. I was also prescribed a wide variety of psychotropic medications. First and foremost among these was the medication Ritalin, which works to calm down hyperactive children while also stimulating the mind and body in adults. Children who suffer from ADHD can benefit from using this medication, at least that's the prevailing wisdom. When taken for an extended period of time, this medicine may cause psychosis,

The Cottages

irritability, and paranoia. Increased risk-taking behaviors are one of the common adverse effects associated with Ritalin use, with a rise in the tendency to act rashly. No wonder I was such a mess!

Recent lawsuits have asserted that the manufacturers of methylphenidate, better known by its brand name Ritalin, and the American Psychiatric Association colluded to construct and promote the diagnosis of ADHD in order to generate a market for it and related medications. Some people want to spread the notion that conditions such as ADHD and Restless Leg Syndrome (RLS) are entirely in one's head and are, in some ways, not actual diseases. This is not the case, at least in my experience as a patient. It is a reality, and it is terrible! The purpose of using Ritalin is to bring behavioral issues under control; nevertheless, the medication also has the potential to increase organizational abilities and listening abilities. It did not have much of an effect on me. The facility's behavior modification tools did what the medications were unable to do. When the defiant part of me recognized that it was pointless to fight them, I behaved, and shortly, I was rewarded and I was transferred from the 'Ward' to the 'Cottages.'

Northville State Hospital near Hawthorn Center

I believe my very first crush was on a girl with long blonde hair who was located in the girls' unit. The hospital's patients were kept in separate boys' and girls' wards. I had encountered her rather frequently, and despite the fact that we had never spoken before and that we never would, I made it a point to be in the vicinity of the lunch room whenever she was around; it was the most exciting part of my day. Never even had a conversation with her, never kissed her, but there isn't a month that goes by without me thinking about her.

There were around seven or eight cottages at the top of the hill behind the main center, and these were intended for patients who had been judged to be trustworthy. Every cottage had its own athletic team, and those teams would compete against one another. Additionally, we did amazing things like rock collecting and rock polishing, which piqued my interest and I became fairly skilled at doing both. When I was there, I also had my first experience with homosexuality. An older boy came to my bunk one night to initiate me into the methods of oral sex (him on me). Because I had never ejaculated before, I initially believed that he or I had damaged something and was pretty frightened; however, I was later informed that it was completely normal. The effeminate young man was both comforting and very gay, although at the time I didn't really know what that was; all I knew was that he was different in some way. We would occasionally run into each other in the cafeteria or at events, but other than a brief nod, the incident was never brought up again, nor was it ever even acknowledged. I came to the conclusion that I'm not gay… so please stop looking at me like that!

My time at Hawthorne was both intense and brief. I was a rather unique case. My front-line doctor, Dr. Galligan, worked with Hawthorn Center founder Dr. Ralph Rabinovich (*left*).

He broke new ground in treating emotionally disturbed children with hyperactivity and was one of the first to draw correlations between sugar intake and hyperactivity. They also found it interesting how I used imagination and fabrications to deal with the trauma of my family breaking up. I thought I was the reason why the family was breaking up and why my dad had to go away. Looking back some 60+ years now I can see a lot of it was just a call for help from a troubled, young lad. I think the overall point I'm trying to bring to you is the fact that if I can overcome, these kind of hurdles and setbacks in life you can too. I know it might be trite sounding but it is true… after all they're generalizations for a reason.

Father Gibault's

After my time at Hawthorn, I went through a period that I like to refer to as 'The Lost Years,' during which I spent time in a succession of homes for problematic youths that were operated by the Catholic Church. It was agreed that Tom needed to move onward in his path, and via my Mom's contacts with the Church and our longtime family friend, Father Frank Burns, a space was found at Father Gibault's School for Boys in Terre Haute, Indiana. This was a working farm operated by the Brothers of the Holy Cross and the juvenile offender residents. They had cows, hens, horses, and possibly up to ten acres of land that was cultivated in corn and other crops. I earned my way and was given the privilege and opportunity to work with a group of Hawks and Falcons. I made it a point to educate myself all about them and their needs. When I was feeding them one day, I remember making a mistake that could have resulted in the loss of one of my eyes. It's improper to take a piece of food and cross it in front of your body while one is feeding a falcon since there is a risk that the bird will attack the person who is feeding it and cause injury. And that's precisely what happened. I grabbed the piece of meat from the tray and brought it across the front of my body. At that moment, the bird, which was agitated since it was time to start feeding it, flailed its enormous wings, and in the commotion, its talon struck me on the forehead directly above my left eye. If it had been half an inch lower, I would be the one-eyed author talking to you right now rather than the person I am. Leasson? Follow the damn directions!

The Nuns of Christ the King would have a rough time keeping up with the Brothers at Father Gibault's, both were tough as nails. One of the primary types of punishment that we were subjected to was being forced to kneel with our faces in the corner of the room. The problem with this was that the floors were made of hard linoleum and I still struggle with back pain to this day as a direct result of the hour-long sessions in which we were required to kneel. The Brothers, just like the Sisters, were of the opinion that corporal punishment should be used, but more on that later. This is the same school that Charles Manson attended when he was a little boy, which is certainly not an honorable distinction.

I've always been the type of person that asks 'why not?' unless somebody else told me I couldn't do it, and even when they did, I believed that if you were able to think of something and you wanted to accomplish it, you could

find a way to make it happen. I have always been this way. One of the years that I was at Father Gibault's, we were watching the winter Olympics. I was a huge fan and liked watching everything from the ski jumping to the downhill slalom, but the bobsled teams were my absolute favorite. My eyes were glued to the television for the entirety of the event, whether it was the one where they lay on top of each other and go down the hill on a small sled or the full-scale four-person bobsled teams. I had no idea what I was getting myself into or how challenging it would be, but I made the decision to construct a bobsled despite the fact I had never done anything like it. My dorm room overlooked the top of a large slope behind the building, and I routinely dreamed of bobsledding down it. They thought I was nuts.

When I originally mentioned the concept to the Brothers, I recall that they looked at me like I had three heads. It took us a few weeks, as well as a lot of insults and derision directed at me, but in the end, we succeeded, and the result was very cool. The do-it-yourself bobsled that we built had a front carriage that could be turned, it could seat four people, it had ski runners on all four sides, and it worked well. The following winter, we used it for the first time, and we had a lot of fun going down the hill. It was extremely quick, roughly twice as fast as a conventional toboggan. The difficult part was carrying it back up the slope so we could start over. But we did.

During this time, my Mom, who really is a saint, would occasionally travel all the way from Detroit on the bus to come down and visit me on the weekends. She would take the Greyhound for the six or seven hour journey; I will never understand where she got the stamina to do that. When I was younger, I recall that I really wanted to go see the new Beatles movie 'Yellow Submarine'. She took me. However, as we were watching it, Mom fell asleep, and I remember thinking to myself, 'Wow, she must be really tired.' In the following months, I discouraged her from coming down to visit since I knew that she was working a full-time job and was responsible for taking care of my sisters and brother… she would simply be too exhausted to enjoy the trip.

At Fr. Gibault's, you were considered a Farm Boy, and the order of the day was to get up with the sun and go to sleep when the sun went down. One of my memories involves an incident in which I was accused of smoking cigarettes behind the barn and then punished for doing so. I told them I was not there and the other students involved also said that I was not present. I spun around just as the Brother was going to strike me with the huge paddle, stared him dead in the eyes, and yelled, "I did not do this!" And he responded by saying, "Well, this is for all the other times when you didn't get caught!" And in response I shouted, "Fuck YOU!" I wasn't able to sit or lay down for several days without experiencing excruciating pain. Even now, I carry the bitterness from being falsely accused and punished. They were aware that if I was caught engaging in inappropriate behavior, I would readily accept own my guilt and the consequences "like a man." To tell you the truth, I have a suspicion that the good Brother had some sadomasochistic tendencies.

When you accuse someone of doing anything, you had better be damn sure that you're correct about it, otherwise you should get ready for the consequences. There is always a reaction, both equal and opposite in kind, to every action… We used to be given the opportunity to go on field trips to the city nearby. There were a variety of stores and one of the shops served as a hardware store. Being the spiteful little jerk that I was, I stole some Liquid Metal, brought it back, and then, when no one was around, I got up in the middle of the night, went to the school building, and put liquid metal in each of the door locks. Come Monday the brothers were not happy. There are some extremely pleasant memories like that, alongside some others that aren't quite as pleasant. If I had done what I was accused of, I would have taken the punishment with no complaint.

St. Vincent's
After three years, it was decided that I would be moved to a facility that was located closer to my family, so I was sent to St. Vincent's Home for Boys and Girls in Lansing, Michigan. The state capitol. It was more like a boarding school situation (primarily for orphans), and during the

Father Gibault
Basketball Team

day, we would attend St. Mary's elementary school
which was located just three blocks away from the State
Capitol. There, I had my very first teacher-student crush
on Sister Rita Marion, a young Puerto Rican nun. She
was my 5th grade teacher and I was acquiring the skills
necessary to learn from and interact with other people,
particularly the ladies.

My sister Elaine, who worked as the head designer for
Jacobson's, a prominent department store in Detroit, she
visited our house one autumn and decorated all of the
bulletin boards using her own time and money. There
were maybe five or six of these bulletin boards in the
home. My sister Elaine was never thanked by the Sisters,
and after she had departed, one Sister said to me, "well, I
bet you think you're special because you've got such a
talented sister, huh?" This memory is seared into my
mind because the Nun never even said 'Thank You' to my
sister Elaine. What a cruel remark to make, and I let her
know how I felt about it. It demonstrated that even if you

do everything right and go out of your way there are still some individuals who will never be grateful.

The home was a few miles away from Saint Mary's school in downtown Lansing, which was around two blocks away from the state capital. It was there that I first became interested in politics. I used to slip out of the school in the middle of the afternoon, stroll over to the state capital, and sit in the gallery to watch our elected

representatives argue about the topics of the day and figure out new ways to take advantage of the people who pay the taxes in the state of Michigan.

While I was a resident at St. Vincent's, it was determined that I required the assistance of a "Big Brother." Ed was a kind person who had been divorced and did not have any children of his own. He worked as a salesman at a car dealership. It turned out that he was really passionate about two things; The first item on the list is Slot Cars; he owned a number of them and a selection of controllers as well. We would go to these slot car centers that had large tracks with ten lanes and when the races started with the vehicles side by side, it was a sight.

Sex was another activity that was very important to Ed. While the two of us were occupying his vehicle, the topic of women and sexual activity was brought up. We engaged in conversation and I asked a few questions about it. He took a paternal approach to the situation, and it was made abundantly clear that this was something that an individual did by themselves (alone) to themselves. It was also made very clear that this was something that everyone did and that it was completely normal and natural. After some time, I recalled that the very first time I tried it, I felt like I was about to pass out. The only other sexual experience that I can recall at that time is when I was serving as an altar boy, and the priest who came to say mass would have 'roaming hands'. His name was 'Farther Michael' and we would engage in a wrestling match, during which he would touch every part of my body, including my buttocks and crotch, and then he'd declare, "It's just wrestling." I never had the feeling that I had been violated and I said nothing about it, and completely forgot about it until I started writing this.

Boysville

After spending some time in Lansing, I was moved to the famous 'Boysville' in Adrian, Michigan. There I became a member of the Marching Band and did well in the role of Drum Major responsible for calling cadence and dancing as I led the band down the street. It was a lot of fun, and it helped me direct my show-off energies properly.

I remember that for the very first 'Home Coming' at the school, I was in charge of greeting guests when they arrived at the main gate and pointing them in the right direction. When my Mom arrived, she didn't even recognize me until I removed the feathered band hat I had been wearing. I have a feeling that she was rather proud of me. The Brothers of the Holy Cross are also in charge of the Boysville School for Boys, which is known all over the world, and it was there that I first became interested in music. As a member of the Marching Band, I was taught how to play the Bugle and the Trumpet. I also participated in Choir, where I acquired the skills of reading music and singing on key.

Because I was having some difficulties in school, I was assigned a tutor rather quickly. She went by the name Miss Sarabini, and I had such a crush on her. I kept dropping hints and making insinuations, and eventually, she caved into what I was suggesting… only a little kissing and fondling, but no real sexual activity of any kind. It was still very hot, and I always looked forward to my tutoring sessions.

At Boysville each residence hall has a 'Brother in Charge,' sometimes known as a "BIC," and ours was the very tall Brother Robert. We had an instant and mutual hatred for one another, despite the fact that we were both from the same state. Over the course of two to three months, the tension increased, and eventually, we got into a fight, during which my thigh went through a window, resulting in 21 stitches. The following week, he was sent

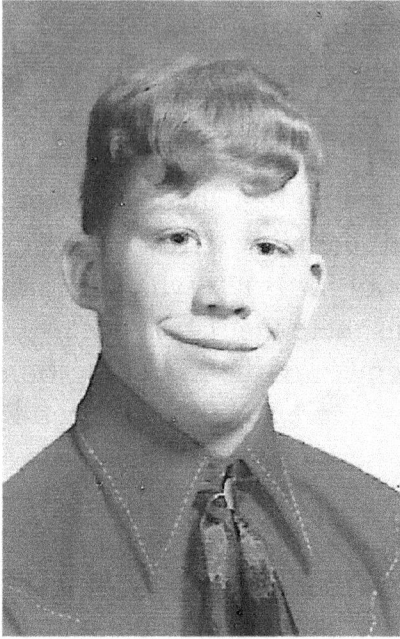

to a parish that was located further up in wilds of northern Michigan.

Derby Junior High
It was time for everyone's favorite juvenile offender to have a homecoming, and everyone was excited! When it came time for me to attend high school, it was determined that I would return home and start as a freshman at Derby Junior High School and later Seaholm High School in Birmingham, Michigan. An upscale suburban community where the neighbors had significantly more money than we had, Birmingham was still a good fit... safe with good schools. The fact that my mother was able to purchase a Townhome there baffled me. It was a relief to get back to the routine of being just a regular student in high school, but it also made me feel a little out of place, so I tried my best to blend in.

When I was in junior high, I made three friends who will last a lifetime. We became good friends and roamed the streets together. Our group included Tom, Dave, and me.

During one of these incidents, my friends and I broke into the school and stole several field hockey sticks. As we were traveling down the railroad lines, we saw a gap in the fence. Because the spot lights were pointed directly into the parking lot, anyone who stood there would have been visible only as a silhouette. I came out from hiding behind the fence, raised the stick to my shoulder as if it were a weapon, and said in a very booming voice, "Hold it! "Get your pants down!" And I emphasized that point twice to demonstrate that I was serious. The man tried to undo his belt, but we started laughing, and so in an instant, he took off toward us, and we ran for what seemed like miles, but he never caught up to us. The man never caught up to us. Just some good, clean, boyish fun that, in this day and age, would likely get you shot and could possibly be deemed a criminal offense. I believe that we scared the guy to the point where wet his pants!

Many years have passed and I've learned that Dave has become a woodworking artist and builder in Northern Michigan, whilst Tom has become John Lennon in the most successful Beatles tribute band in the Midwest. Pete 'Grack' Washburn, who now lives in Italy, was another person from Derby who was a friend for life. He's one of the most upbeat and optimistic guys I've ever met. When we were in high school, we both played in bands, and after graduation, he joined the United States Navy and served there for 20 years as a musician. We chat rather frequently despite the fact that he is far away.
These individuals have had a significant impact on my life. Jerry, Tom, Dave and Pete extended the invitation to call me friend, and I took it… and that was more than 50

years ago! Sadly we don't seem to have men like this anymore. Ever talk to a 18 year old? It's scary. One wonders if 1933 happened now would Generation X, Y or Z rise to the occasion? I have my doubts. Maybe I became spoiled from the hero's I saw on the big screen?

☖

Fighting' in the Streets! The Riots of '67

I remember a warm July Sunday morning as though it were yesterday. I was living in Farmington at Grand River and 9 Mile Road. My bedroom window faced south towards downtown, and as I looked out, even as far away as we were (20 miles?) I could see huge clouds of black and gray smoke rising in the distance. We had no idea what we were seeing until my uncle, a captain on the Detroit Fire Department, called to say a major riot was underway and to stay home. No sooner had Uncle Johnny hung up than the phone rang again, and it was my Uncle Russ, a Detroit Police Officer, saying the same thing. We Irish are mostly police officers or firefighters because, when we first came over on the boat, these were really the only jobs we could get. My grandfather told stories of seeking work and signs being put up that said, 'Irish Need Not Apply'. So even from an early age, I understood prejudice and bigotry.

After lengthy vacillation by local, state, and national leaders, armed soldiers—both US Army troops(!) and the Michigan National Guard—were deployed in many areas of the city. It was a good thing too, because 2-3 days later there was a Tiger game we had tickets to! The 4-block area at Michigan and Trumble around Tiger Stadium was like Switzerland's neutral territory. Crime in the Tiger Zone was almost nonexistent. As far as I can recall, it has always been this way. At the time, I really had no idea where all this might lead. I was just a kid, and all I knew for sure was that this was bad.

We had friends down there at St. Luke's, so my mom, who was truly fearless, took me and a family friend and loaded us into the station wagon. Then it was off to the store and then down to the parish rectory and our longtime family friend Father Frank Burns. All was fine there, and I remember one thing crystal clear. We had loaded everything in, and Father was walking out the door to the church next door. It had been decided that the doors to the church would be opened and that Fr. Burns, 'Padre' (that's what we called him) would say Mass. So he was headed out the door, and I ran up and gave him a huge hug around his waist and said, "Padre, are you going to talk with God?" And I will never forget that he bent over and, in an almost whisper, said, "No, Tommy, I am going to *listen.*" Nothing in the parish was touched during the riot, and the church stayed open 24 hours a day until it was all over. When we got back home, we discovered the rumor mill had been cranking full tilt. Supposedly, a crowd of angry black rioters were marching down Grand River Avenue towards Farmington and threatening to burn the suburbs down. Others were going to poison the regional water treatment system. Both of these and many other rumors turned out to be total bullshit. By the way all my favorite concert halls went untouched during the riots.

In my youthful ignorance, I wondered what could have provoked one of America's largest civil disturbances. "Why are they doing this? They are only burning down

their own neighborhood!" Later, I came to understand Detroit's brutality against blacks by a nearly all-white police force; high unemployment and widespread poverty; segregated and substandard housing; and terrible public schools that led to a pervasive sense of hopelessness, powerlessness, and anger in the city. This spilled over into riots in the summer of 1967 in America's 8th largest city.

But the riot—or rebellion, as some have called it—also set in motion decades-long reconsiderations of the long-suppressed issues of race, poverty, joblessness, and despair. The uprising also accelerated "white flight" out of town and provoked a long-lasting image of Detroit as an unstable, potentially violent city. We sometimes forget that Detroit was only one-third black in 1967. It is well over 80 percent black today. Sadly, even today, much of Detroit looks like the riot happened yesterday, and many,

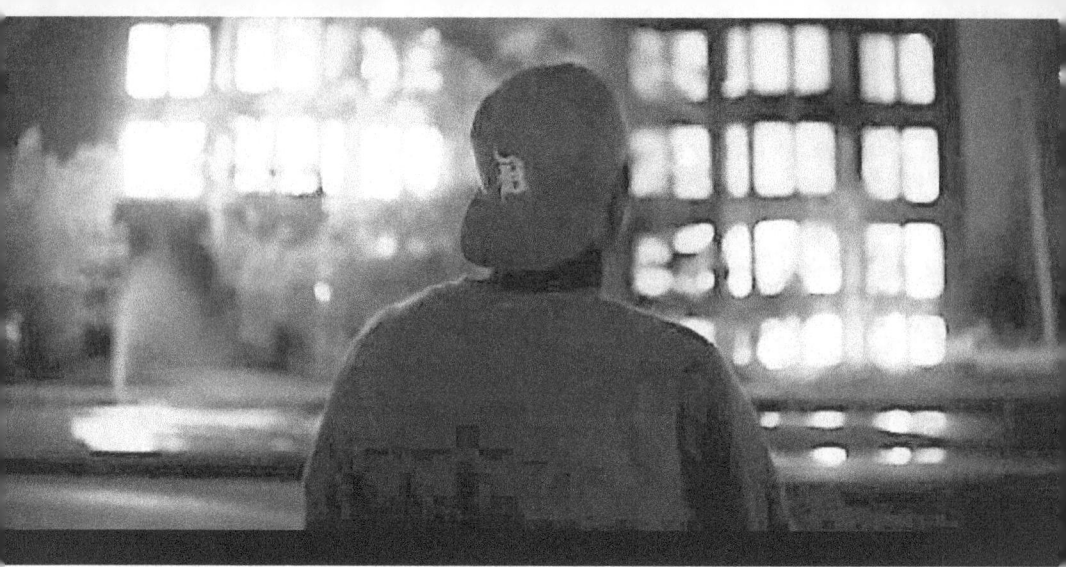

if not most, of the problems that were the precursors to the event then are still factors in the city today.

On July 23, 1967, the worst event in Michigan history was happening right around the corner from our house. It was the first time I can remember actually feeling unsafe. In total, the 'uprising' lasted five days with 43 deaths, 1,189 injuries, and more than $350 million in business and property damage. Even today, the events of the early morning hours of that hot July night when a police raid on an after-hours drinking place exploded into the Detroit rebellion are etched in my mind.

1967 Detroit Riot Stats
43 Deaths
1,189 Injured
7,200+ Arrests
400+ buildings destroyed
$45+ million in loses

☣

Chapter 2

Poor Boy, Rich Kids
Keeping Up with the Jones

"Rich kids who write songs about food stamps always piss me off!"
Song Writer Neko Case

After years of therapy sessions, it was time to unleash me on the world and for me to rejoin normal society, and make my way through the minefield of high school. At the outset, it was clear, at least to the bullies I encountered—the rich kids whose dads worked for GM or Ford and who were able to drive to school in a new car —that I was from the wrong side of the tracks. With my blond afro hair and round glasses, I looked a bit like a cross between Angela Davis and the cartoon character Funky Winkerbean. The teasing and hazing was relentless. But I began to embrace the fact that I was a little different, and I had come to believe that the problem was theirs not mine.

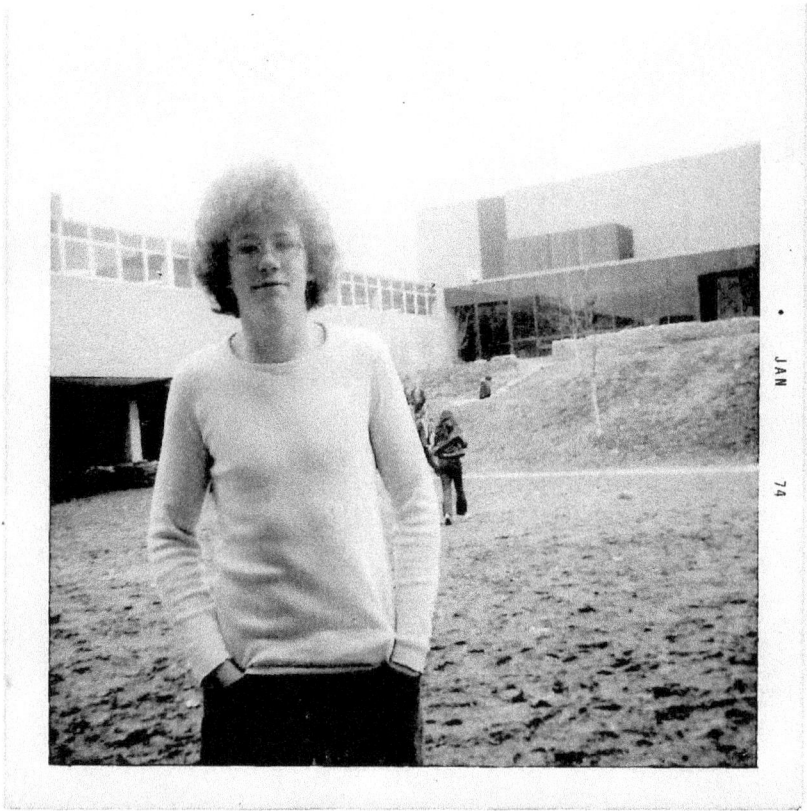

It was during this time that I started traveling to Ann Arbor, going to the free concerts in the park, and hanging out at John Sinclair's Rainbow People's Party Headquarters on Hill Street. I ingratiated myself and started volunteering to help run sound and lights for the free concerts in the park every weekend. Mostly I just carried amps from the back of the truck to the back of the stage, but I got to be backstage or at the sound board about halfway out in the audience. I was also at the Free John concert and got to see John Lennon do the song 'Give Ireland Back to the Irish'. These were heady times, and this is where I began to be politically aware and active, mostly against the Viet Nam war (both my brother and brother-in-law were in direct line for the draft).

The powers that be retaliated against outspoken John Sinclair, who had created the White Panther Party, which later became the Rainbow Peoples Party. He had been set up and busted for two joints, and he was promptly put into Jackson State Prison. Lesson? The powers of America do not like to be challenged, and I came to believe that cannabis was a gift from God and that the marijuana laws of this nation are crude, cruel and unjust. If one did not know any better, one would think it was just a money-making scam by the government and to give it the ability to hassle people of color. They didn't like what Sinclair said, so they trumped up some charges and put him in prison. Par for the course.

I believe in the American free enterprise system. So, being the young entrepreneur that I was, I needed a source of income. In addition to playing gigs with the band, which paid little, I became a dealer of cannabis. Just enough so I could smoke for free. There was this park near where we lived called Hines Drive; it was actually a series of roadside parks out near Novi and Northville. One of these parks along Hines Drive featured a large hill. We would divide up a pound of pot, put the ounces in our pants, and then make our way to the top of him. If the cops ever came, we could see them from a mile away and take countermeasures. The contraband would come up with us on one side, and we would descend the other side with the Benjamins in our pockets. Many times the guitars and blankets would come out, and it would be a Woodstockesque happening right there on the lawn. More than once, I saw young couples making love on the grass like it was a 1968 love-in. Fun times on the lawn in the sunshine.

Birmingham's affluence featured lots of restaurants and a shopping hub with tons of shops with the latest fashions. Another advantage to living there was a concert venue called 'The Palladium' just off Woodward and 15 Mile Road, where soon-to-be national and international acts would perform for $10. The Birmingham Palladium opened in 1969 and closed in 1972, and it could only seat about 1200 people. It was there I saw Badfinger, The Bob Seger System, The Velvet Underground with Lou Reed, Big Brother & the Holding Company with Janis, and Grand Funk Rail Road, just to name a few. I didn't realize at the time how big these bands would become. Nobody did. When I was younger I went with Mark Coca via the Grande River Bus to the Grande and the Eastown as often as I could.

And, of course, there were all these fantastic Detroit bands that nobody outside of Michigan had ever really heard of: The Frost, The Gang, SRC, Savage Grace, Frijid Pink, The Rationals, and so many more. The great thing about it was, of course, the music, but also the fact that I could walk to the side of the stage and watch the sound man and lighting director work their magic. Many of these acts were only starting their careers and would continue on to become world-famous platinum recording artists; others would just be local 'stars'. For a kid just in high school and 17 going on 25, these were groovy times.

It was the time of suede, silk, and velvet, with white folks dressing up like they were pimps down on Woodward Avenue. Even I purchased some blue suede shoes with 4" heels, which made me about 6'9! Like any teenager, I needed money, and some that was legally mine. I got a part-time gig at 'The Village Green' a head shop on Woodward, above which, luckily, were the new offices of America's favorite rock-n-roll periodical, CREEM Magazine. With a Boy Howdy nod from the journalism gods, I wound up as a runner for the likes of editors Dave Marsh and Dave Di Martino. It was weirdly straight out of the movie 'Almost Famous', and I both had a blast and learned a lot. My gift for producing high-grade bullshit was paying off, and I was able to talk my way into places and situations that would terrify a mere mortal adult, let alone a teenager.

Somewhere along the way, Tom discovered he could sing and do so on key, so soon it all became about making the band and rock-n-roll. Now, Detroit has always had some truly great musicians, and the suburbs around Birmingham and Bloomfield Hills had a plethora of players to jam with, and with my blue-eyed soul, I did.

I became friends with one of the most popular guitarists in the area, and while I never really played with him, I did roadie for him at a few gigs. He always had the best pot, and you could get a 4-finger lid of Columbian for about $35–40. His Mom worked, so we hung out a lot but while they were jamming in the basement, I was upstairs fucking his sister, or at least trying too. And later, I think he found out because he was distant after that, so I think he knew. And she was the aggressor, not I; she was a 'big' girl with dark Middle Eastern features. And I remember it well, as it was the first time I really tried different positions.

I recall that he was the master of the backhanded compliment, and the teasing was relentless. I often got the feeling that they kept me around just to be able to have a verbal punching bag. That was OK with me, though, because the music was what I was all about anyway. And as their 'roadie' and #1, at least I was always able to sit front row or be backstage. He was very talented and went on to play in some fairly major Detroit bands before moving to Los Angeles where he fit right in. He was a hard one.

In the summer of 1974, I put together and was the promoter of our own local music festival. It was held in the outside theater at Oakland Community College in Farmington Hills. My band performed, and we had five other bands with about 1000 attendees. We even made a few bucks. I wore my 'Kiss' boots—knee-high boots with 4-inch heels and silver lighting bolts up the side!

Seaholm High

In high school, my office was in the E-wing John (Bathroom). I spent many hours there. We had a radio for jams and a small cooler for drinks. A 4-finger ounce of Columbian went for $40. We actually installed a lock that we could activate in case teachers or staff came looking, but in 3 years, that never happened. And perhaps that's one thing that is so different in today's schools... I mean, we smoked joints in the John, but we would never think to bring a gun, a knife, or anything like that to school. It was just so out of the box for us to even thing of that. That's why when my grand niece tells me that she has to walk through a metal detector in order to get to class, it is so foreign to me. When they do active shooting drills, I wonder what we're really teaching our kids. It's little wonder they're so scared and paranoid most of the time.

America's Only Rock 'n' Roll Magazine — CREEM

Getting back into the routine of regular life, things went along swimmingly, and I fell in with a pretty good group of people. I discovered I could actually sing on key, and we started a band that became popular... Scarlet Omen.

After a few years, it was decided that we could not afford Birmingham any longer, so my Mom moved us to the more affordable Farmington. It was hard to leave my friends, but what I could do? I became a sort of conduit and connected players from the Birmingham regions to the Farmington, and Novi areas, and vice versa.

Farmington High School

In my junior year, we moved to the more affordable town of Farmington, about 10 miles away. It's a cute little suburban town with its own high school and movie theater. The Farmington Founders Day Festival is an annual event that draws thousands. The school is above average. One of the classes that a lot of people took

Blue & White

Farmington High School   Nov. 7, 1974

Scarlet Omen from left, Mark Lapinsky, guitar; Dave Hilton, bass; Tom McAuliffe, lead vocalist; Joe Kalek, drums; and Mark Leonard, guitar. They will be performing along with their special guest star, Brian Shepard, November 8, 8-11 p.m. here at F.H.S. Tickets are $1.25 in advance, $1.50 at the door.

because it was supposedly fairly easy was Choir. It was taught by an older gentleman named Mr. Floyd, and about the second week of school in September, me and my other friends in the back row decided that our goal for that school year was to drive Mr. Floyd right out of his mind. The goal would be that he would have to leave on a psychic or psychiatric sabbatical, and I'm not proud to say we almost accomplished that. We would sing off key on purpose and substitute music sheets for nonsensical musical documents. One time we put clothes inside the stand-up piano so that when you hit the keys no sound came out, and then we nailed, with just two nails, the top of the piano shut so that you couldn't open it. The poor man stood there for almost 20 minutes trying to figure out why no sound was coming from his piano. It was hilarious, and later he even said so.

And straight from the movie Sister Act, we put glue on his chair. All in all, he took it in stride and with a fairly good sense of humor. Two years later, when we graduated, I made it a point to go back to him and thank him for teaching me to read music. He was very gracious but indicated that he was happy that my cohorts and I were moving on. We don't pay our teachers enough money, and maybe we should start giving them flak vests! If you go into a school today, you might notice that some teachers have perfected a way of writing on the blackboard without turning their back on the class. Sadly, the reason why children in schools are undisciplined and unruly is the fact that they have no guidance at home. Funny that I should think that now.

In Farmington, I created a new band with myself as the lead singer. Dave on Fender bass and vocals, Joe on drums with dual bass drums, and Mark Lennard on guitar and vocals. The band started as Tarkus and migrated to being called 'Scarlet Omen', playing parties, school dances, a few weddings, and bars in the NW Detroit area. One highlight of my high school senior year was when my band participated in the annual student talent show. We played three Beatles songs and an original tune; we did not win, and the following Monday I got suspended because we had a couple of beers backstage. We did, however, come in second place.

One major gig we played was on New Year's Eve 1974 at the Pontiac Theater. The venue was a once gorgeous art deco theater from the 1940s that, although it had seen better days, had been converted to a concert hall like The Grande Ballroom in Detroit. The opener was a unique one-man band named 'Brian Shepard'. He did a amazing 45-minute set. He would sit at a double bass drum set with a Gipson 335 guitar in his lap and a head mic. Using a device called an Echoplex, he would lay down about 30 seconds of a riff and then be able to play over the top of it. He put out a huge sound, and he was well received.

Then there was my band for a 50-minute set. We played 3 originals and the rest were covers, from the Stones to Santana (we had a conga player that sat in for 2-3 tunes) to Bowie to Arrowsmith. The crowd dug our set. Then a DJ played dance music. Then the 'headliner' was a group named Tantrum From Livonia that did boogie blues music and whose lead singer seemed to be a smack head. It was entertaining. We kicked out the jams and played to about 500 people who we had dancing in the aisles.

After the gig was over, we did a little NYE partying of our own, and it was just shy of 2 a.m. that we discovered that the security guy had split with some girl and there was now only one exit. We were trapped like rats! So we began to lug our equipment up the long aisle and made our way through the lobby to the vans waiting curbside under the marquee out front. All the while dodging the few remaining drunks who had passed out earlier in the evening but were just now waking up. Oh joy. So while breaking down the equipment, I noticed a young kid walking up the aisle with $500 worth of cymbals. I have never seen the drummer move so fast in my life! He tackled that boy in row 65 and began to have a talk with the wayward young youth, who moments later limped away. But we had survived the night, so life was good. Each man got $100, and the sound/light guy got $50. 1975 was off to a roaring start but by the end of the year I would be sailing for Uncle Sam.

In the out door...
My buddy Jerry is a world-class drummer who has played everything from punk to rock to big band and jazz. Actually, he's so good, he's a percussionist! When we were teenagers, he was always very popular, as he had a car, so we would pile in and hit the gigs. Many a Saturday night would be spent with my head hanging out the back window, puking my guts out. And we had a taste for the ganja. To break into the small time so we could smoke for free, we needed weight. He knew a guy who knew a guy. We met him at an A&W drive-in on Woodward, just off 13 Mile Road near Botsford Hospital.

After driving around for a few minutes and smoking a sample, we were directed to a smaller, two-story 1950s apartment building. We gave him $1000 for a pound of the premium. There was no reason not to trust him because, after all, he was vouched for. He said he would be right back. We waited in the car, and after about 10 minutes, it began to dawn on us... But you know how when something bad is about to happen, and you don't really want to believe it's going to happen? So you say to yourself, 'Nawwww, he's just running a little slow, that's all.' Fat chance! We had been ripped off but good.

After walking to the back of the complex, we determined that he walked right through the lobby and out back to a waiting car. Pretty slick. We drove around for an hour looking for his car and tried to get up with the guy who turned us on to him, but never did. It was a hard but necessary lesson, and each of us pointed the finger at the other. But in the end, we realized it was our own fault. "Face it, Flounder, you fucked up... You trusted us!"

Later that Fall I learned that I had a talent for putting words together and in telling stories. I started thinking I could be a writer. It was my being runner-up in the school's Poetry contest as a Sophomore that gave me the idea:

October

October had come again
and that year it was sharp and soon...
The fraudsters early burning the thick green on
the mountain sides to mast brilliant hues of
blazing colors. And pain in the air with sharpness,
sorrow and delight... and with October.
Sometimes and often,   *there was warmth by*
day, an ancient   *drowsy light, a*
golden warmth and   *pollinated haze in*
the afternoon. But   *over the earth there*
was the breath of a soft   *and covering frost...*
And exult and see all the men who were returning,
a haunting sorrow for the buried men, and a
nothingness for all those who were gone and
would not come again.
It was October...
/ / / /

My high school English teacher, Mrs. Mauer, informed me that she recognized writing talent in me and that I ought to give some thought to pursuing it. But I had already made up my mind that music would be my muse (which, looking back, was a decision that almost certainly insured that I would live in poverty). However, I was going to keep this thought in the back of my mind... I had no idea how significant this idea would become in my life until much later. You can't always predict how significant an experience will be on your life or how influential the words of another person will be until much later. When it came to writing I was a natural.

It wasn't until about two months before I graduated from high school that it was discovered that I was missing a half credit in "Physical Education" (often known as "Gym"). Therefore, being the blarney stone kissin' Irishman that I am, I connived my way into convincing the school to let me backpack, and while I was on my way to California I would keep a journal of my trip and hikes along the route, and then turn it in for the required half credit. This allowed me to fulfill the requirements for graduating. The trip was scheduled to last between two and four weeks, but it only lasted between seven and eight days instead because we rapidly became proficient at getting rides. Before I knew it, we were in the wild, wide west and southern California. I did in fact finish the work, handed in my log, was awarded the credit, and was given permission to keep the high school diploma that I had obtained a few months before.

As a result, I found myself in the city of Angeles, with the wacky notion that I would somehow find a way to work in the film industry or the entertainment business or something. Because Cerritos Junior College in Northeast Los Angeles offered classes in both theater and radio, I decided to enroll there. In addition, I studied acting at Los Angeles Community College also known as LACC. I obtained a job cleaning the college pools—there were three of them—at 4-5am, five days a week so that I could put myself through school. It was challenging for me because I am and have always been a night owl. In addition, I did not waste any time in getting involved with the college radio station, and after I had been there for a semester, I was given my own show on Monday, Wednesday and Friday from 2:00 to 6:00 p.m. The show was called 'The Motown Music Review' and it featured not just music from Motown but also Blues, R&B, and even some reggae. I named the show after the label since I was from Detroit, and because it was the music I was familiar with and enjoyed. After a few months, thanks in large part to my outspoken nature, it quickly became one of the most popular shows on the station's schedule.

A few months later, I was called into the office of the Dean of Student Affairs, and it was brought to my attention that the college's Black Student Union had a problem with a white boy like me doing an all black music show. As a result, after much back and forth, it was decided that I would be taken off the air, but in exchange for not making a fuss, I wanted and got some compensation. I was given a full scholarship and was relieved of my early morning responsibilities to clean the swimming pools. Thank God! The most essential thing, though, was that I had acquired the ability to negotiate! I was by myself in the city of entertainment, and I was resolved to find a way to make it in the wild and wacky world of show business… or die tryin.

⊗

Chapter 3

Hollyweird
Hells Angles Ride Naked Down the Boulevard

"There's no Business like Show Business!"
Ethel Merman

Living in LA was indeed an eye-opener for this middle class Midwestern boy. Even being from Detroit, there were some things I did not know. I found that, indeed, Hell's Angels did ride naked down Hollywood Blvd. I had purchased a 750cc Norton Commando and was enjoying not only having a motorcycle but being able to ride without a helmet (dumb, I know, but…). I was doing everything my Mom would not allow me to do back in Michigan. I got my 8x10 B&W promo pictures made and began to make the rounds of auditions like thousands of other young, starving actors.

One encounter that I shall never forget was at a large talent agency on the other side of Burbank near NBC. I was the last interview of the day, and I sat on the sofa in anticipation with my black and white 8x10 glossies. The assistant director came out and sat down next to me, rather closely. He was a large, well groomed obviously gay man and impeccably dressed. He put his hand on my leg and basically said I could have the part if I had sex with him! I was to return at 11 p.m. wearing only a bathrobe. Upon further inquiry, I found he didn't really want to have sex… what he really wanted was to rub oil all over my entire body. I was learning that Hollywood was a very freaky place. Needless to say, I politely declined and I did not get the part!

The Cops Came

Winters are brutal in Michigan, and so I got a lot of calls from folks wanting to visit me in the California sunshine. My lifelong friends, Pete 'Grack' Washburn, whom I mentioned earlier, is a bass player who I've known since junior high school and have jammed with many times. He decided to come out from Detroit and pay me a visit. I was living in an apartment that looked like many of the ones in southern California—sort of a converted motor lodge with apartments above and below and a postage-size pool that was at best a health risk. Well, with the motorcycle and guitar, as well as a fair number of almost out-of-control parties, it soon became very apparent that I was no longer welcome. As if to reinforce that fact, the landlord called the police, and they came right after a visitor fired up a bong. As the cops pushed their way through the front door, Pete began to play his Bass faster and faster—it was like some old Keystone cops reel. It was very funny, just not at the time. The downside was that they made us pour about an ounce and a half of pot and all the liquor down the toilet. It was a very sad sight. They told me in no uncertain terms that if they had to ever come back, they would be taking me and everyone else to jail. I took the hint and began looking for a new place to live.

So the apartment, which looks like something out of the Rockford Files, was right along the major boulevard, about 2 miles from the college. When I had the first party, it was a fairly tame affair, and even when the manager came, it was sort of a housewarming. The second party, about 2 months later, was louder, and the neighbors called and asked us to keep it down to a low roar. A month after that, at the end of the semester, we had a loud rock duo, and because it was close to campus, a lot of 'students' came… and not to feel uninvited, the cops decided they would stop by too.

And I need to say that, being from Detroit, these were six of the nicest police officers you would ever want to meet. As they again rushed into the large apartment my good friend Grack was not even noticed; in fact, I don't think the cops even talked to him the whole time. Some folks just have a way about them that is like Obi-Wan Kenobi… 'You don't need to fuck with me; move on.' My other buddy, Chris Eppert, a short 5.5', 25 year-old guy with shoulder-length hair, also came to CA to visit me. He was 'Mr. Party' and always came home with drugs, women, or both. He had a heart of gold, later joined the Army, and died in a house fire. Sad. I miss him all the time. He was a man who knew how to party.

So after about 2 hours of loud rock-n-roll (is there any other kind?) I looked up from the couch, where I had been talking to a very pretty young lady, into a virtual wall of blue. Officer Johnson pulled the plug on the stereo right out of the wall. (Right in the middle of 'Heavy Music' by Bob Seger too!) I was not surprised to re-learn that because my name was on the lease, I was basically responsible for everything! That included the large bag of pot that was left on the coffee table. It was quickly confiscated, and Chris, who seemed to think he was going to be able to somehow talk the cops into allowing him to keep it (?), was escorted into the bathroom and was forced to flush about two ounces of Columbian Red down the toilet. He was quite depressed for the rest of his visit.

The cops said that they had talked to the landlord/manager and that it was strongly suggested that I find a new place to live sooner rather than later. The manager later told me that if I got out by the end of the month, she would 'let me out of the lease' without penalty. I moved out a week later but would only turn the key over with the return of my deposit, in cash—no harm, no foul; time to move on down the road.

During this time I also fancied myself a surfer, and after some basic reading, watching, and learning, I was up and going good until I broke my 9' long board on the pilings of the Huntington Beach pier. At night I ran sound and lights for shows at Knotts Berry Farm (a local amusement park), and during the day I would go to auditions and try my hand at surfing. After a while and a few job changes, I wound up sweeping floors on the lot at Universal Studios and basically living on noodles and rice. But in my delusion, I was somehow in the 'crazy business of show" It was hard times, and I remember getting a letter from my Mom basically saying, it's time to come home. I wrote back, "And what, give up my job

in show business?!" I decided to give it another 6 months, and after wearing out 2 pairs of shoes when fall came and nothing positive had yet to appear on the horizon, I was about to throw in the towel and head back to the Motor City. I was discouraged but still determined to make my way in life and I was not beaten.

I never could really figure out what I wanted to be, probably because of my ADHD. My mind always goes in 50 different directions, and I could never really set a goal or decide what I wanted to do for a living. It's the curse of the multi-Talented I guess. My interests are as varied as oceanography and history to entertainment and motion picture production, Comedy is also right up there. I've always been able to make people laugh and when you do it and things go right, there's no feeling in the world like making an audience laugh. And there's no pain greater than telling a bad joke in front of several hundred people.

Cali Girl

I had met her on the beach at the Huntington Pier. She was gorgeous with long blond hair and had an ass like an onion… cause it made me want to cry! After a chat, she invited me to a party up in the canyons, past Mullholan

Drive and west Hollywood. It sounded good, so Saturday came, and I took my Norton motorcycle up there. The house was something out of a movie, and for good reason: it was owned by a daytime drama actor who had been on TV for years but had recently left the show over money. He was evidently now involved in producing big money porn in the valley.

I was 19 but looked like I was going on 25. As the Norton made love to the curves of the road suddenly I had arrived. In the driveway was a new silver Porsche 911 and through the floor-to-ceiling glass walls of the home, I could see a spotlight-lit pool under the eucalyptus trees with two women and a man swimming naked. As I walked up closer I recognized one of the women as the girl from the pier. I nodded to myself and I immediately got an erection just thinking of her. A knock on the front door and it swings open… The man climbs out of the pool, shakes himself, puts on a kimono, and walks into the large living room to say hello. A kid smoking a joint walks in from the other doorway with an armload of wood and begins to make a fire in an enormous freestanding copper hearth like in a ski lodge.

He sits down cross-legged across from me on the large Afghanistan carpet near the fire. He's a muscular dude in his late-20s, clean-shaven with auburn hair to his mid-back. He could pull his hair back and fit in with any corporate boardroom and he probably did. He's also a multi-millionaire responsible for about 30% of pot distribution in the Midwest, including my home state of Michigan. The kid comes back with a bottle of expensive

French Petrous wine, vintage 1961. He walks over and puts on a record. $5000 worth of gleaming Macintosh and Altec Lansing sound turns on with presence and brilliance. It's Dave Mason's song, 'Only You Know and I Know'.

"Who are you, and what do you do?" he inquired rather sternly.

"I'm Tom, and I'm a friend of (and I motioned toward the girl in the pool), and I'm ahhh, a writer," I offered. In an offhand way I explained that I want to do a story on him and the Pot business.

"OK, dig 'Tom the Pen man'... (instantly I had a nickname), there are five Panama Reds in Detroit alone," he says with presence and brilliance.

"Which one are you?" I ask.

He takes a long drink of wine—why sip it when there's plenty more?

"Thee Panama Red," he said proudly.

Only you know, and I know,' ... pours out of the stereo.

As if schooling a student, he leans in and says, "Dig this. If the man picks up a runner and threatens to put him away for good unless he tells them the name of his connection, let's say he cracks and says, His name is

Panama Red!' And they say, 'Which Panama Red? There are five of those fuckers!' So the man is right back where he started when the runner says, 'Gee, I don't know, fellas, thee Panama Red, I guess'. He stops and rolls a joint. Continuing he says, "So as I was saying before I interrupted myself... I was sitting in my lakeside retreat before a crackling fire mashed fruit flies and..." The phone rings, and it's a friend of Red's, 'Billy the Zigzag' and for some reason the guy wants to speak with me! I hesitate but take the phone and he starts...

"Bill the Zigzag sez hello to Tom the Pen Man!"

"Same to him," I said, "who am I speaking to?"

"The person on the other end of the line from you... I'm from the mitten too," he said.

"I mean, what's your name?" I probed.

"Don't have one," he said matter-of-factly.

"You don't have one?" I continue.

"It's like when you meet a heavy person and you say, Hey man, and they say, 'Bob, Tony, or something, but they don't tell you their last name because it's just too fucking bourgeois to have a last name, OK? Well, we were into this thing recently of like, "There was this dude who was lending people money in Detroit and you knew him only as 'the Snake... Better get the money out from under the mattress, mother, because one of the Snake's boys is going to be here at 7 PM!' Mr. Zigzag continues. Yeah, well, all of a sudden he's busted, and they got his 'ol picture in the news paper big as shit that it says, 'Carmen "The Snake." Holy shit, so that's the snake… Let's go down to the DA and pitch a bitch! Put a name with a face and kiss your ass goodby!"

'Cause you know that I mean what I say,' sings Mason.

"Well, we've been having the same sort of trouble with pseudonyms here, man. The cops pop you, and you get busted for everything your nicknames have ever done!" he continued. "So while it may be too fucking bourgeoisie to have a last name, it's just too fucking mortal to have just a first name or nickname, so a lot of us are just ditching the whole fuckin name thing entirely as counterproductive," he said. "You can call me 'Zag' if ya want," he said, passing me the joint. "Besides, the only thing your name is good for is so people can find you and so you can be famous and make a lot of money," he said. "Well, I've got money, and I have no wish to be famous nor found… Anyone who wants to find me either better fucking know me, in which case they know where I live, or don't know me, in which case he's a condensed pig fart and had better have had the last rights before arriving at my picturesque hippie commune. There are two former humans who showed up unannounced and who now only exist as notches on my Magnum Ray Gun," he stated. "And as far as making connections and money, that depends on my *not* being famous, OK? Maybe you need a name, man. But I don't," he said.

"Isn't it confusing trying to deal with people who don't have names?" I naively ask. (I've still not seen pier girl.) "No, it's kind of liberating really. It's like when you call the phone company about your bill and the lady always tells you her name, but you don't really care, do you?," he asked without needing an answer. "People I deal with don't really care because the dope trade is like the phone company. It's not who in particular you're talking to that makes a difference," he said. "it's whether you're plugged in at the right place in the network!"

"Swell… So ah what's happenin'?" I say trying to get a relationship going.

"Well, I'm glad you asked me that question, Tom the Pen Man, because the reason I'm calling you is… bye now!"

Click.

And I'm left sitting there holding a dead phone… Boy, journalism sure is fun. About 5 minutes later, the phone rings, I pick up and it's a familiar voice…

"Sorry about that… I'm at this rather plush restaurant using a payphone, and there are some people waiting to use the phone, so I let them because I discovered that when I was impatient to use the phone, I found myself studying the features of the dude who is keeping me waiting, and I don't want nooooobody studying my damn features," he explains.

"Well, at least you're not paranoid," I offer.

"Yeah, well, funny thing, I am paranoid, and that's why when I heard you were there at Red's, I wanted to rap with you. I figured if I told you about a scene some sort of scary people ran on us last week and you published it somewhere, me and some of my friends would feel a little safer at night. I mean, if they wanted to ice us, they would have to ice you too!" he said.

"Gee, thanks!" I respond. So this was what this was all about, they wanted and needed some insurance and protection by putting this story in the media, which is I guess where I come in.

"You're welcome. So the faster you get this story out, the safer we will *all* be. Capeesh? Besides, nobody's gonna ice a writer! Even an unknown one," he said.

"That's comforting," I said holding back any hint of fear. Suddenly the guy from the pool returns with Pier Girl in tow, and he pulls a small brass box from underneath the couch, opens it, and begins to scoop a significant amount of cocaine onto the glass table top in front of us, cutting it into long lines with a large knife. He proceeds to roll up a $100 bill and snort the lines. I am offered but decline, and I learn that the top-less woman from the pier is named 'Carri' with an 'i'.

I continue on the phone with Zag, ignoring them and continuing, "I won't burden you with all the details, but let's say word got around that a lot of us were getting together at this place called Walled Lake outside Detroit. Personally I didn't want to go because I'm kind of antisocial anyway, and the idea of the entire embroidered Afghan money-belt set of Motown partying together begins to sound a little too much like a set-up for a remake of The Little Bighorn," he said. "But I went because I heard this particular dude was going to be there, a legendary dude named…"

"Wow, he's even got a name?" I ask flippantly.

"Got to have a name to be a legendary smart ass. Don't interrupt!" He scolds. "But anyway, it's like not the name he called himself… It's the name other people call him… Besides, if you stop butting in, I'll tell you his name, and then you can tell me if it's the name he called himself… OK?" he asks.

"OK," I respond.

"The World," he said dramatically.

"What?" I ask.

"The World," he says again in a more serious tone.

"What about the world?" I ask.

"What about him? That's his fucking name man… 'the World'.

"You mean like 'The Snake'?" I ask.

"Yeeeeeeah man… do you well to look into this."

Dialtone.

It was the strangest phone call I had ever received, both before or since. Because I took notes on it, I have a very distinct memory of it. To make a long tale short, Carrie left with the guy, Panama Red passed out in a lounger by the pool and as a result, I discreetly strolled outside to my 1969 Norton Commando motorcycle and rode off into the cool Southern California night. What Zag wanted was for me to get his story some coverage in print to give him some sort of safety factor. I was not able to do so and I was never able to follow thru on the Pot Distribution story. But after that, I never had to stress about a cannabis connection ever again. It's nice to have friends!

During my time at Los Angeles Community College, where I studied Acting, I came to the realization that many stereotypes about the west coast are, in fact, accurate… The Hells Angels are known for their notorious practice of riding nude. People in California do not have concerns about drowning in the ocean in the event of a catastrophic earthquake. And another thing I discovered to be true was that despite the fact that I ended myself sweeping floors at Universal Studios, in my head I had always imagined myself working in the entertainment industry. My experience has shown me that if you want to believe something desperately enough, it is not difficult to convince yourself of a false reality. And that's California, always open to innovation and delusion.

After some time, I came to the realization that bad fortune had followed me there and that, despite the fact that I did not know what lay ahead of me, I wanted to go back to my hometown of Detroit in order to figure out what my next step should be. After learning that my friend Mark from high school had enrolled in the United States Navy as a photographer and was required to report for basic training at the end of the month, I boarded the first available flight to Detroit in order to wish him well before he left for bootcamp. We partied.

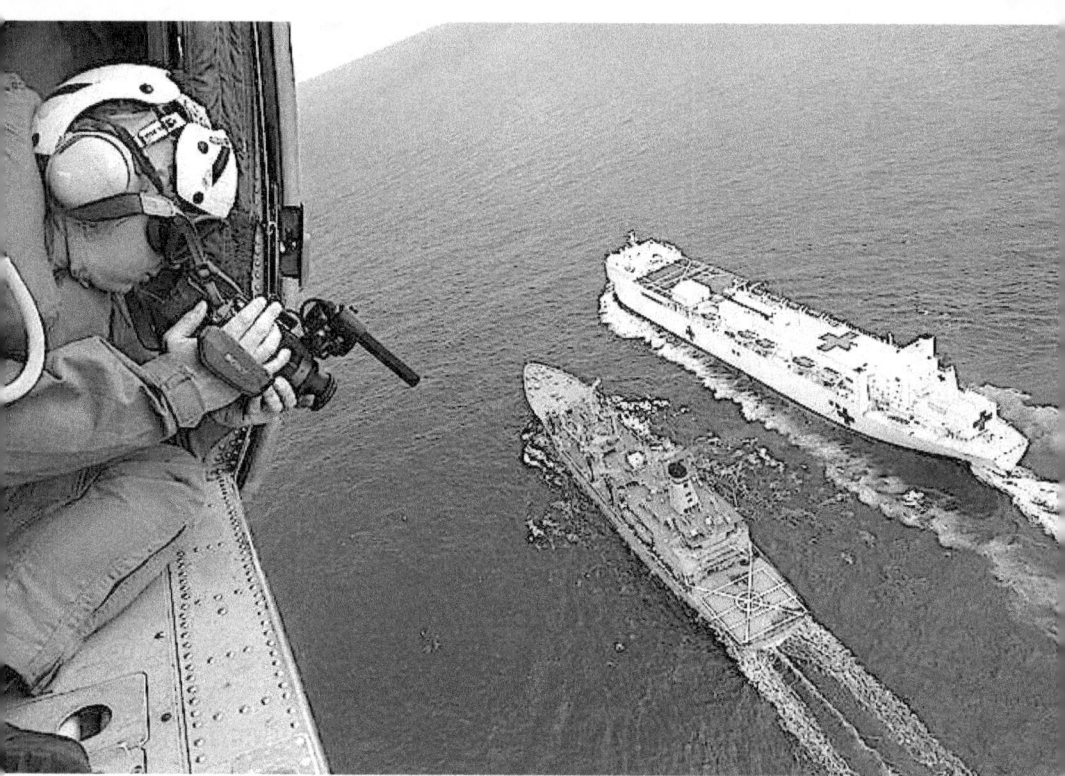

Chapter 4

Anchor's Away!
From Happy Hour to 4.0

"Damn the torpedoes, Full speed ahead!"
Admiral David Farragut, USN

Sometimes, when somebody's back is in a corner, it leads them to making bad decisions and sometimes good decisions. In the winter of 1975 the economy, at least in southeastern Michigan had gone right into the crapper. I tried for months on end to get a job with no end in sight. One of my good friends and an awesome guitar player, Mark Hargraves, who I went to school with at Seaholm, had just joined the Navy as a Photographers Mate. This

sounded very interesting to me and I soon found that I really had no choice. So with no other prospects in January of 1976, our nation's Bi-Centennial, I raised my right hand to defend our nation. About three weeks later, I got on a grey government bus and was sent to the Great Lakes US Navy Recruit Training Command just outside of Chicago with approximately 6 feet of snow on the ground. I had wanted to go to San Diego but was told that was not possible. The next nine weeks were some of the most grueling of my entire life, before or since, both physically and mentally.

I've always had an aversion to authority and this was no different. I have a couple of vivid recollections from my time there… one such memory is when I first arrived. I got in trouble walking across the Quarterdeck of our "Compartment: (our dorm). The Quarterdeck was a lobby area of the dormitory that was treated like it was the Quarterdeck of a ship, part of that was a square area that was painted blue and it was to be treated as if it was water. No one told me that! I was halfway across it when a booming accented voice stopped me in my tracks.

"Oh my God! *Where the fuck are you going Boot*?! Do you think you're Jesus Christ and can walk on my water? Get down there and give me 20!" he screamed. I could only do about ten push-ups and that made my new friend even more livid. He grabbed me by the scruff of the neck and marched me out in front of the Barracks where there was a six to eight foot high pile of snow. There were two shovels and I was instructed to move said pile from where it was to about 6 feet over, and I thought to myself... 'Well there must be a good reason for this... they need it moved because they were going to, I don't know, do maintenance or something like that. However, when I was done a few hours later, I found that this was their idea of punishment as I was told they wanted me to put the snow back from where it came. I was sore for three days and never wanted to see a snow shovel again.

My Company Commander, the guy who was sooooooo welcoming at the Quarterdeck, was a 20+ year naval veteran. Senior Chief Machinist Mate Emilio Acosta was a tough Filipino who spent most of his career below decks in 120 degree engine rooms. He let it be known that if you want to serve in his beloved Navy you were gonna need get by him first. Inspections at Boot Camp were a daily part of the drill. During one such personal inspection, we had to get up around 4:30am and the inspection was at 5:30. As I told you before, I'm not a morning person, my years of working in nightclubs and radio made me want to rise about the crack of noon! I was always a night person... at any rate we got up, it was the middle of the winter, and it was snowing outside. We put all of our uniforms on, got into formation, and marched over to the main inspection hall. The inspection team, which was one main guy and then two guys following behind him, one with a Clipboard marking everything down and the other as backup, started to inspect. Of course, being out front next to the Recruit Petty Officer Cadet (RPOC)... I had become the

Assistant RPOC because I could call cadence 1- 2 -3, 3-4. I was one of the first to be inspected!

The inspector came to me, stood in front of me, and suddenly burst out laughing. I did not see what was so funny, but I started laughing as well, and when that happened Senior Chief Acosta hit the roof! I could not understand what was so funny and then after the Inspector had moved on to the rows behind me Acosta was behind me and started whispering in my ear, "God, damn you McAuliffe... you fucking cost me a perfect score... when we get back to the compartment I am going to mash you like you've never been mashed before! (A mashing is when you're forced to do calisthenics) You're going to be sweating blood! When I'm through with you you'll wish you joined the goddamn Army!" I had no idea what he was talking about or why he was so hot under the collar at 6 o'clock in the damn morning I only knew that I was in deeeeep shit. Later I found out that I wore my T-shirt inside out *and* backwards! To this day I don't know how I did that and Senior Chief Acosta true to his word, took a large piece out of my ass. When we got back to the Compartment, and after his tirade that evening, I was sent to a event called 'Happy Hour.' It is a nightly occurrence that happens about 7 o'clock each evening when you are taken over to a gymnasium/indoor drill hall for some personalized one on one 'instruction'.

So we marched over there, and we were left standing in formation for probably almost an hour, and then the 'fun' began... Four or five Drill Instructors (DIs) descended upon the group, and for the next 90 minutes, they gave commands for forced calisthenics, to the point where many of those who incurred infractions were throwing up. There was definitely nothing happy about it.

Everything done in the Navy is done for a reason. So they even taught us how to fold our clothes. There was a specific method and logic to it. The logic being that storage on board a ship is limited and finite so if you can take up less room with your clothes, it's a good thing as you can stow more gear. So they even taught us how to fold our T-shirts in a process called "skinny, fat, fat, skinny" because after you were done when you looked at the T-shirt on the side, the folds were skinny and then two fat ones and then another skinny one. I fold my T-shirts that way even today. Everything has its place, everything in its place, was the clear lesson. Ship shape.

I met a lot of great people while I was in the Navy, and some of them are still good friends even to this day. In bootcamp, we had a lot of characters, one of which was Kevin Boogaloo

from Kalamazoo, Michigan. I swear that's his name. Kevin was as fucked up as the day is long and he could not march to save his soul. We would say, 'Kevin... left face to the rear... March!' And he would freak out and spaz out in all different directions. All that was fine if for nothing else than the comedic value, but there was a more serious problem at hand... Kevin snored. And I don't mean it was some light snore... I mean when this boy snored, walls moved! Well about the third or fourth week of training, the guys decided that they had had enough. We needed some way to stop the snoring but we couldn't just beat the shit out of him.

So a devious plan was put in motion. First one of the sailors snuck a banana out of the chow hall, now anybody who has seen the movie, 'Full Metal Jacket' knows that having food in the compartment is a huge no-no. But we didn't care this had to be addressed so that the guys can get some damn sleep. So they snuck the banana into the compartment and that night after lights out when Kevin started snoring three or four of us got up, peeled the banana and put some shaving cream on it. Then we snuck over to Kevin's bunk. We put the fruit in his mouth moving it back-and-forth a few times and then a large black guy from St. Louis named Bunky, who was hung like Adonis, pulled his pants down and stood next to Kevin's bunk. His jockey shorts around his ankles and his large member in full attendance, Kevin woke up, touched his chin, saw the white stuff there and assumed the worst. He literally jumped up and ran out of the compartment and outside into the snow screaming all the while. He never snored after that... but I don't think he

slept very much the rest of the time he was there either. And he did proudly graduate with us a few weeks later.

I was fortunate, and through some lobbying efforts after bootcamp I received highly sought-after orders to the Atlantic Fleet Combat Camera Group. In fact, I was the last enlisted person to be ordered into the command, which was then migrated to the Atlantic Fleet A/V Command. It was a new Navy, and they didn't like the word 'Combat' anymore. The command was in Norfolk, Virginia so I went out and purchased one of the very first Renault 'Le Cars' in the USA with cash and after 3 weeks leave, I made my way to my first duty station.

Years later the Doctors and I came to the realization I had Post Traumatic Stress Disorder (PTSD), but it wasn't really from jungle firefights in combat, I've never experienced those, my PTSD came from shooting pictures of dead bodies, mostly from aircraft accidents and perhaps more accurately from developing those pictures and seeing those images come up from being invisible when they were in the 'soup' (which is what we called the photo development chemicals). One vivid memory I have is of an Admiral's daughter, who's airplane had gone down in Chesapeake Bay and she had been in the water for five or six days so half of her skull was gone. Sadly, I see those pictures even now. We had a lot of great and exciting assignments however; we covered the sinking of the Argo Merchant ship off Massachusetts. I flew above the ship as it was going down and shot film and pictures. We documented the invasion of Grenada in 1983. We did some things for NASA, but mostly, I remember spending six months with the United States Marines' 32nd Marine Amphibious Unit and doing a film about amphibious landing warfare and SEAL endeavors. Later, I also participated in creating a educational film called 'Until the Seas Run Dry' about US Naval history.

All in all it was a very productive time for me and I quickly rose through the ranks to PH2, an E5. I was never ships company (part of the crew) and after three or four years I was selected to attend a special DOD program at the University of Syracuse where sailors basically get out of the service for a year, you can even grow your hair long, and study mass communications and journalism at the University of Syracuse in upstate New York. Their 'SI Newhouse School of Mass Media' is considered by many to be one of the greatest learning centers for journalism, newspaper and magazine production in the world. I had a great time, learned a lot and basically chased every woman I could find.

Looking back it seems like most of my time in the Navy was spent in school. I did the basic A and B school at Naval Schools of Photography in Pensacola, Florida, a town that I had that I have grown to love and returned to some 50 years later. Then I went to Defense Information School at Fort, Benjamin Harrison in Indiana where I learned about Broadcasting, Video and Audio production. It was invaluable training that's unavailable elsewhere.

My time in the Navy was both intense and rewarding. I had many assignments that were both special and dangerous. I earned my gold Aircrew wings and could legally wear a Naval leather flight jacket. I looked pretty spiffy, but Officers, especially junior ones, didn't like an enlisted puke wearing what they did. I met some of the biggest assholes I've ever met in my entire life, but at the same time, I met wonderful people and made lifelong friends in the Navy. For example, my friend JO1 Rich Yankou, a Journalist First Class, is a lifelong friend. I get a Christmas card from him every year. He is USN retired now and lives with his wife in Japan. What other job can say that? It's like the old ad used to say; "Navy—It's not just a Job– it's an Adventure!"

I loved flying. I used to love hanging out of a chopper at 150 MPH and documenting the Navy SEALs and the amphibious operations of the United States Marine Corps. I've watched and filmed huge armadas conduct amphibious operations and it is really something to see. The backs of ships open up and all these little amphibious units, like ants, come out of the back of the ship and head towards the beach. I also regularly got to fire the M-16. Because I was a photographer and kind of a different or a special case they treated me well which was always amazing to me. By the way those heroes in the SEALS are some of the most down to earth and quiet individuals you'll ever run a cross. They never talk about ops. Show me a guy who sits at the end of the bar and blathers on about his time in 'the war' and I'll show you a liar. Courage and bravery need no megaphone.

Being 'Aircrew' meant that I also got to fly in all sorts of planes and helicopters; A4, F4, A1C Hummers, COD planes, C-141 cargo planes, CH-46, CH-53, and UH-1 choppers, and more… but the coolest was being the first enlisted personnel to fly in the F-14 Tomcat at NAS Oceana off the coast of Virginia. We shot some wonderful pictures of the base and of 3 Tomcats flying in formation past the Wright Brothers memorial at Kitty Hawk North Carolina a few hundred miles to the south. These images were printed up as posters and were hung in recruiting offices all over America. One of the last maneuvers was to get a fish eye shot of the whole base. This would require the aircraft going up to about 15,000' and then going inverted upside down so I could shoot down thru the canopy and frame the base. I got the shot, but after the maneuver, I lost my lunch (threw up). When the flight was over, I started walking away down the fight line when the crew chief came up to me,

"Where *you* goin Sailor?!"

He handed me a bucket with rags and said, "You messed up my plane... please remove your throw-up from my multi-million dollar aircraft!" It took me 2 hours.

It wasn't all fun and games; during one amphibious operation off the coast of Spain one of the amphibious vehicles sank with seven Marines drowning. During the rescue/recovery operation, they wanted everything documented, and it was up to me to do so. Another incident occurred when I saw the CH-53 helicopter flying in front of us, have its rotor touch the side of the canyon, and go down with a squad of Marines in the back. Six Marines gave their lives for our nation that afternoon. I had to go and take pictures of the bodies, they were mangled beyond description and I still have visions of it. As we've discussed, while I do suffer from PTSD, it is not nearly as bad as those who were actually there in a fire fight or air accident. For me the affliction is almost a secondary one with nightmares of what I saw through my viewfinder, and what I saw coming up from being invisible in the soup when the prints were developed. And the soup was what we called the chemicals that are used to develop the prints in the dark room, so after thousands of dollars and years of therapy and various drugs, I still have nightmares. And I will also say that Cannabis has made a remarkable difference in my life and should be legalized and authorized by the VA for medical treatment of PTSD but that's another book…

Is my affliction debilitating? Sure. Do I want compensation? Nope. Would I change things? Not on your life. I am proud to have served and the adventures I had were truly remarkable… at least to me.

After four years in the fleet on the tip of the US Navy's photographic spear at Combat Camera I was selected to attend the military program at Syracuse University… It's a special Department of Defense program where one photographer or journalist is selected from each of the five services, including the Coast Guard, and they leave active duty and for one year become a civilian student studying with some of the best minds in Media.

Two examples readily spring to mind. There was John Mitchell, formally of the Associated Press and UPI, and one of the toughest professors in News Journalism. I would routinely get papers back with grades like 'G', 'H' or 'U'. We would be deducted one grade for every misspelling or punctuation error and an error of fact was an automatic F. He was interesting in that he was of the old-school… where journalists pounded the pavement and then hammered it out on large, jet black, Royal typewriters. The writing was in the wall, and adapting to the new way of computers and digital dissemination was underway. I both loved and hated him, but I sure learned a lot. Another wonderful professor was Dr. Mario Garcia who was more than anything, an artist and designer. He redesigned all kinds of newspapers and magazines across the country, including USA Today and Forbes Magazine. From him I learned that it's important to have some style while delivering the information and the more you can make your layouts interesting and engaging the more readily the information will be absorbed by the reader.

Of course basically being a civilian was a real treat. I had my own apartment, which I was supposed to be sharing

with another military student, but who was married and decided to get an apartment of his own with his wife, so I had the place all to myself. And I am here to tell you I made good use of it. There are not a whole lot of women on ships, so being near and available to the opposite sex was a new and exciting experience for me, and I made the most of it. I think in the course of the year I dated seven or eight different women. The other cool thing of attending Syracuse University was how one came in contact with all kinds of different people and cultures from around the world.

For example, my next-door neighbor was royalty from the nation of Jordan, complete with Turban, long white gown, the whole 9 yards. He was a wonderful man and unfortunately security requires that I'm not reveal his name here. He had two cars one was a Corvette, and the other one was a Trans Am. He used to let me drive it. When the end of the school year was approaching, I was honored that he held a special Middle Eastern 'Fete' (dinner) for me. He gave me my own white gown and a 'Ghutrah' a traditional suede Arabian headdress. I

looked good. The night of the special dinner for 'Sailor Tom' came, and other Middle Eastern students came, but no women. They had a long table, but it was flat on the ground, and then the servants came with these huge trays, and the trays had rice, roasted vegetables, chicken, and lamb, they poured this white yogurt-like gravy on it, and it was delicious.

One sort of embarrassing but funny things that happened was actually eating the food. I noticed when we were sitting down, and of course, you have to sit sort of cross-

legged on the floor, although there were pillows all over the place, I noticed there wasn't any silverware anywhere to be seen. There were lots of cloth napkins just no forks, spoons, knives… nothing. So I just hung back and watched everybody else and I noticed that they would basically rip off a piece of chicken or lamb, grab some rice, and use their hand to form it into a little ball and then eat it in one swift motion. So one learns by doing and I reached out with my right hand to grab some chicken, and my host nudged me and he whispered to me; "No no the right hand is the *toilet* hand…only do left!" Indicating I should only use my *left* hand. In that case, one either learns how to be ambidextrous or one starves. It was a night to be remembered, and both the company and the food were phenomenal. I learned that we really are all the same and want the same things out of life. One thing the Prince use to say became one of my favorite mantras: 'The dogs may bark… but the caravan moves on!' Set your goals and march towards them.

One other incident is worthy of recollection. While at Syracuse…the USA was having a problem with Iran when Khomeini was taking over. One of the guys in our class, from the United States Marine Corps, had worked in counter intelligence. I don't know all the particulars, but what I gathered was that he and his team would go into these areas, some of which were in enemy hands, and try to ferment insurrection and sow civic confusion. I don't know it for a fact, but I believe that he had received orders while at the University to do the same, and as you see by the picture, they held a rally and he burned in effigy a picture of Khomeini. I believe the goal was to get young people upset and riled up against Iran, who had previously captured and held American hostages. So his command had followed him to Syracuse and had him organize an anti-Iranian protest. He did so, and it received national media coverage and was very effective in my opinion and from a counter-intel standpoint.

All of this was in preparation for my returning to the fleet as a Photojournalist with the special Naval Enlisted Classification of NEC-8148. At the time, there were only 23 of us world wide. After much prodding, cajoling and a bottle of Johnny Walker Red whiskey to the Detailer, the guy who determines what your orders will be and where your next Duty Station will be, I got what I felt was the very best orders in the fleet. I was to be a Photojournalist and staff member of All Hands Magazine in Washington DC. It was a monthly magazine that talked about the US Navy's programs, commands, and sailor achievements… sort of like a magazine version of Stars and Stripes. After graduation from Syracuse and some leave time, I made my way to the Pentagon, and although prestigious I hated it. It was stodgy, huge, and a political minefield.

During the brief time I was there, I had the unique opportunity to testify before the US House of Representatives Committee on Military Affairs. They were taking testimony and investigating the fact that Naval Enlisted Personnel had not received a pay raise in almost a dozen years. I brought up the fact that many of our active duty enlisted members, especially in the lower echelons, had to be on food stamps, or some sort of public assistance. They weren't paid enough as the cost of living in Washington DC is quite high. No one ever told me, but I definitely got the impression that my testimony ruffled a few feathers, and some saw me as badmouthing the Navy... And I know that to be the case because about three weeks later, I was told that I was suddenly being transferred to a new publication. Normally, one would be upset and see it as a demotion. But the new publication, to be called Campus Magazine, was about the Navy's education programs.

The United States Navy operates the world's largest schoolhouse, with more sailors, going to school every day in the Navy than in any other organization on the planet. This new monthly magazine was going to cover all that. Best of all, it was in Pensacola, Florida, where I had attended the Naval Schools of Photography years before. I love that town. So, while it may have been a demotion to some, I was on cloud nine and looked forward to not only working on the new magazine, but also hanging out on the Emerald Coast.

Like many in Combat Camera Group I got married, and I got divorced. Her name was Theresa and she could be Dolly Parton's twin. Theresa's 6 year old daughter and I had a very special and loving relationship. I liked her Mom a lot too. At my next duty station, the Chief of Naval Eduction and Training (CNET) things went along swimmingly for a while. Then we got a new supervisor, JO1 Johnson... What an asshole! He's the kind of guy that makes people not want to re-enlist, and when I let it be known that I was not going to do so, the rancor and hazing was endless. It was insults, it was articles being sabotaged, missing paperwork, etc.. The Navy was upset that it had spent millions training me and I was gonna walk. But my mind was made up to forge a life of my own and away from Uncle Sammy.

In 1983 at CNET I came up positive for marijuana in a random urinalysis test. The year before, I had been named 'Sailor of the Year', but now because I was suspected of having smoked a joint in my living room while I was off duty, I was somehow deficient and a pariah. Before, when I was quick with a joke or to chat people up in a positive way… folks liked me. Now, the Master Chief wouldn't return my calls, none of the officers wanted anything to do with me, and I was persona non grata everywhere. I went from a being 4.0 sailor to being a Shitbird (a technical Navy term for someone who is in trouble). I only had to deal with all this for six months before I was honorably discharged.

I never looked back and immediately started college on the G.I. Bill at Pensacola State College. I was studying Broadcasting and Writing and one of my Professors was the legendary John Teelin from WCOA radio in Pensacola. He taught me a lot and got me my very first radio gig at TK-101. I did overnights, fill ins and ran the Sunday morning shows like Kasey Casem's Top 10 Countdown. Not great but at least I was on the air and I was finally in charge.

⊛

Chapter 5

Da College of Real Life
Hard Knocks and Good Luck

"Hard Times Require Furious Dancing!"
Actress Alice Walker

Determined to use every last dime of the GI Bill I had earned so I enrolled in Pensacola College's Broadcast Arts program, during which time I was also an intern at local radio stations WCOA-AM (Newstalk) and TK101 FM (AOR). Radio got in my blood, and I was going to try to be a on-air radio personality. But it would be a tough nut to crack! After 3-4 semesters at Pensacola Junior College it was decided that it would be more cost-effective if I moved back home to the mitten, which I did just in time for the fall semester.

I enrolled in Oakland Community College in Farmington Hills, part of the Oakland University system. The school had a 100-Watt student radio station that was being closed down mostly because no faculty member nor student was interested in keeping it going. I told the Dean that I was! He liked the fact that I was older and a veteran. So, I began the chore of bringing it back from the edge of oblivion. I became the Station Manager of WORB-FM at Oakland Community College. I held a fundraiser, and we improve the signal transmitter and antenna... I actually once climbed to the top of the 200' antenna tower to adjust the antenna. We played alternative music, and our playlist was cutting edge. For example, we were the first radio station in Detroit to play U2, Los Lobos and Rhythm Corps. I once talked to on-air personality Arthur Penhollow long-time afternoon drive jock at WRIF-FM, the major station in Detroit at the time, and he told me that his Program Director followed our playlists religiously. We stayed on top of all the new groups from Europe and around the USA. After 2 years I left the station with new equipment and a better signal. Graduation came and my Mom finally got to see her youngest son in Cap and Gown. I was graduating with as AA in General Studies, and at the podium the Dean told the audience that I had almost single-handedly saved the college radio station. WORB-FM is on the air in NW Detroit even now.

So it was a fun life with school by day and DJing in Nightclubs by night. I was taking a full class load… had a weekly radio show on WEMU and DJ'd from 8 pm to 2 am five nights a week. It was fairly lucrative and a whole lot of fun. And while there were lots of very pretty women about, it was made very clear to me that 'No Muffin Tops' need apply. That's what they call a guy with extra flab around the waistline. Sadly I found it was me!

Once I got my AA degree, I continued on towards getting my BA degree at Eastern Michigan University (EMU). Located in Ypsilanti right next door to Ann Arbor and the U of M campus, Ypsi-tucky is a working-class blue-collar community with many working at the local Ford Motor plant. I got a cheap upstairs flat across from the park, it had a small fridge and microwave, and rent was $400.

I was doing weekend overnights at WHYT in the major market of Detroit and then at WIBM 94 Gold in Jackson, Mich. so I was doing professional Radio while I was still a student. I once asked one of my professors over coffee in a honest and unguarded moment for him... "You know most of these kids will never have a career as a major market on-air radio personality... right?" I asked softly. "Tom, we have no right to steal a student's dream, and besides, despite what some think, we *are* here to make a little money!" he said. It was one of the most honest admissions I have ever heard.

MUSIC RADIO 1450
94 Gold FM
WIBM
Box 1450 • Jackson, Michigan 49204
Phone 787-1450

While at EMU I helped design and open as the main DJ, a bar called CJ Barrymore's, a mega nightclub that holds more than 1000 people in 10,000 Sq Ft. of audio, video, and lighting effects it was one of the first clubs in the area to mix music videos. It's a disco heaven!

The End of the Beginning

I sat in the car my bare hands tucked tightly beneath my body cradling my thighs. The engine fought hard to stay alive and warmed itself as I stared at the delicate frost crystals clinging to the windshield. It was early the sun still struggling to rise as I put the car in gear and headed down the road to work.

Theresa wouldn't be there when I got back. I somehow knew that. She never was. She would be off somewhere with her daughter, playing softball or watching TV. It really didn't matter... she hadn't been there for him for a long time. Even when they were together... They were apart. They are drifted apart what seems like ages ago when she decided she could give her time and money but not herself... She was too fragile, or was it selfish, to share that. It happens, I thought, and life goes on. My brain curled into a silent shrug as I pressed on the brake waiting for the passing train.

Once I believe we were going to make it. I doubted if she ever did. Still, I remembered how we had loved in the beginning. Stealing a moment here, an hour or two there. The long walks, the quiet talks and the Sunday afternoons on the beach. They had touched tentatively at first, physically squirming with childish a light and mentally connecting gently but firmly onto each other. Oh how they were shining. It had never been like that for either of them, before or since.

But even then, I realize now, something hadn't been quite right. "I'm not good enough for you", she insisted from the start. "You deserve someone better. Maybe you'll get lucky." I tried to treat it as a joke. I Tried to convince her she was wrong. Eventually the word stayed away. But the feelings never did. And later, she wouldn't let me share responsibility for their lives together. Only the bad times. "I messed it up" I would declare. "I blew it," blaming himself became a pass time.

My breath vaporized against the window, shredding the car in a vacant gray, and turning the windshield foggy. It was like a bad fairytale, I thought. I had made it all come true. No one else. A horn sound from behind, the train had passed, lumbering hesitantly out of view and into the hazy morning. I turned up the Radio, stepped on the gas, and continued the journey towards the court house. Life goes on I thought as the light turned green and I headed towards the courthouse... and sadly my first divorce.

Chapter 6

Master of the Airwaves
On-air Musings from the Tragically Unhip

"It's not true that I had nothing on... I had the radio on!"
Marilyn Monroe

I'm a recovering DJ. I was an on-air radio personality for
15 years, working in markets from Kentucky to Detroit
and ultimately Florida, working in multiple formats but
notoriously on Overnights as 'The Jammer' in the CHR
format. I was also a central member of the semi-infamous
Z-Morning Zoo in South Florida during the days of beard
stubble and pastel blazers with the sleeves rolled up. Don
Johnson had nothing on me. After a short time where U-
Haul and I were on speed dial I had quickly moved up
the ladder from mid to major market radio; WIBM-FM,
WWJ-AM/FM, WKTG-FM, WXZZ-FM, WMMZ-FM,
WHYT-FM... town to town up and down the dial, I was
a 'voice for hire'.

Yes folks, I was the Florida on-air personality who was
suspended for a week (without pay BTW) for suggesting
that all my listeners turn off everything electrical in the
house, except the Radio, during the execution of serial
killer Ted Bundy in January 1989. Bundy was in state
prison in Stark, Florida, within signal range of the station
and the rumor was he listened to the show. The Station
Manager, who was one step this side of a Nazi, was not

pleased and hit me with a unpaid week long 'vacation'. Next thing I know the local media is calling me for interviews, and there's a listener petition and there was even a rally to have me reinstated. It was a 'Save Ferris' event and a wonderful promo for me and the show... almost as if it was planned (wink wink).

To me Radio is about Community. While I was working at a station deep in coal country, a place where the tune 'Big Bad John' was a frequent song on the request line and incident occurred that illustrates this. The community was the bedrock of middle America with hard working folks whose kids were listening to and calling up to request songs whose lyrical content was equivalent to 'Rape your Father, kill your Mother, burn the house to the ground!' Young girls, 14 goin on 25, who would cruise by the station... which had a large picture window that looked out onto the street so you could see passers by... and they would often cruise by and flash their breasts, which was always nice. One wondered if their Mom and Dad knew.

The jock with the show just before me (3-7 pm) was like many in that business... under the delusion that they are actually in show business. 'Tom Davis' was making a move on anything female and by any means necessary. He had this group of guys call 'The Vatican' who would sit around and brag about 'all the tail they had scored' and was just one of those guys who are constantly on the make with no thought above the groin. Almost every man has gone through this phase of sexual insanity.

I had moved to the area, deep in coal county at 'The Kentucky Giant' and it was the 4th time I had moved in 18 months. This one was to teach me a tough life lesson. My transplant included bringing my girlfriend Susan, a wanna-be DJ, with me which, as involved as I was with my career, I can see in hindsight that was a mistake. Tom Davis, who pulled afternoon drive before my shift had a

large, long-haired rug he would keep rolled up next to the console. He was a young mid-20's with testosterone coursing through his veins and thinking he was all that. He had a habit of fucking young girls in the control room while long songs played... only too late did I find he was having sex with my girl friend while I was on the air. When I found out and as I did not want to be held responsible for her... I sent the girlfriend back to her mother in Michigan. She was livid (both the mother and the girlfriend). Susan eventually became a DJ and cruised the airways in Michigan and the northwest—small world. Looking back, it's funny to me that what I thought was true love turned out to be nothing more than sexual infatuation. Live and learn.

"I'm sorry Tom it's something that just happened," Susan whined explaining her betrayal.

"Oh really, it just happened that his dick found his way into you? That just happened by accident is that what you're tellin me?" I asked. "I don't know that I could ever trust you again maybe I never could. But that's fine… Pack your stuff! I'll take you to the bus station and once you're safe and back home with your Mom in Michigan, if you want to come back down here and be his whore, you're certainly welcome to do that." I said. Naturally she was angry, but so was I.

"You're gonna make me go back home rather than just let me move in with him?" She asked incredulously.

"You're damn right! I promised your Mom that I would take care of you while you are down here. I'm responsible for you so I will return you to where I got you," I said. "and what you do after that is up to you. And Susan? For the record I really did love you. So I just want these to be the last two words I will ever say to you… Fuck You!" I walked away towards freedom, leaving her on the bus for Michigan and her Mom.

I saw Tom Davis the next day after I found out, and I made it clear to him that my first inclination was to beat the shit out of him, but that would not solve the problem and that I was a professional. I further told him that I wouldn't be talking with him again and I didn't. One of the things he told me that really hit home with me was that, "I never said I was your friend" and he was right. When I thought back, he never profess to be my friend, and I felt like such a fool for wanting to be a friend and have a friend like that. Live and learn they say, but he was exactly right... how many people in your life do you think are friends, but really are just acquaintances? A true friend is pretty rare. They say that a friend is somebody that you can call and will come bail you out of jail.... But a true friend is sittin' on the bench next to you!

And in the words of the immortal, Lieutenant Colonel Frank Slade; " Well, gentlemen, when the shit hits the fan, some guys run, and some guys stay!" Being on the radio is an intimate form of communication with the ability to directly reach the listener. It was late on a spring Thursday night, about 9:30 pm. The listener request line had been ringing via the blinking light for about 5 minutes when I decided to pick up. It was not a song request. It was the Girlfriend of a Viet Nam vet. He had been up for two days and was threatening to 'do something bad', and she said he had a pistol. I could hear him raving in the background. Despite my better judgement I asked what branch of service and lucked out when she told me he was ex-Navy. I told her to out him on the phone. I did not know what I was going to say, and I said a quick prayer that God would put the right words in my mouth so that I would be of service.

"What?!" he barked.

"Sailor what are you doing? Stand down! I don't know what the problem is but you are scaring everybody including a woman who loves you... and as you're ex-Navy like I am... I damn sure know you are better than that," I said. "Where did you serve?" I asked.

"I'm a river rat, Boatswains Mate served in the Mekong of 'Nam," he said. "But its all gone to shit and I can't take it anymore!"

"I'll bet you can," and I let that sit there in the silence for a moment. "Hell, if you can put up with the Navy's bullshit, you can deal with anything life can throw at you," I chuckled, trying to lighten the mood. "You know that sometimes it's hard to see thru a squall to your port."

"Ya know I was able to control multimillion-dollar equipment (in the Navy), and now employers don't want to pay me to flip fuckin hamburgers! The bills are sky high, my girlfriend can't take my shit anymore and my back is against the wall," he shared. "I'm gonna break!"

"Well my friend tis always darkest before the dawn and your gal called the right number and this Navy vet and your favorite fuckin DJ is gonna get you some goddamn help and right quick!" I asserted. "What's your favorite band?"

"AC/DC?" he offered.

I cued up the bands great tune and let it rip; 'It's a Long Way to the Top… if you want to Rock-n-Roll!'
"Just remember brother and I know it sounds lame but it all starts with one step and you just made it! Hang on…" I offered. I had no idea what to say I just kept praying.

I got an agent at the Veterans Crisis Center on the other line and explained to the people what was going on and then merged the two lines so they could talk. Long story short the Vet Center arranged a $500 emergency grant so that the young couple could keep the lights on, and a crisis counselor spent time talking him down and then came and met with him the next day. Six weeks later, I got a call from her, and she said he was doing well and had landed a job at a local business… she asked that I play her a song, and I did... it was the Beatles and 'It's Getting Better All the Time'. I was very proud and spent the next week patting myself on the back. We need to do more for our veterans, the #1 homeless population.

Radio, when its done by an actual human being and not some pre-recorded machine, also helps keep the community safe. Later that summer I was getting ready to go off the air at midnight. The station was one of a few that was off the air from midnight to 6am. At about 11:15pm the phone rang at the same time an alarm in the newsroom went off. When something Civil Defense related occurs the alarm from the town, county or state goes off with a beep and a red light starts flashing as information comes across a teletype machine. I put on American Pie, our longest record, and went to see what the commotion was.

A 23-car train carrying tankers with caustic acid had derailed at the other end of town and a cloud of this deadly gas was forming. I looked at the weather report

sheet and it called for 3-5mph winds that could and would blow it directly back towards town.

The Civil Defense (CD) system had been activated and residents were ordered to remain indoors and close all windows and doors putting towels in the cracks to seal themselves inside. The only problem I could see with that was the fact that we had a lot of senior citizens in order homes with no Air Conditioning. The phone lines exploded. I called the News Director and he didn't pick up so I left a message. I called the Program Director… same drill. I went on the air and read the prepared statement from the state CD folks. I then explained what had occurred and most importantly that the station and I was here and would remain on the air and that we were all in this together. I was alone and it was up to me.

The station did not really allow DJs to air phone calls for fear that the caller would say something offensive. There was no 7-second delay switch. But in a moment of insane clarity I decided this was an exception and that the community needed to communicate with each other and by extension with authorities who could monitor the broadcast. So, for the next eight and a half hours, I took calls. We got the Fire Department Scene Command on the line for a direct update. I called our sister station's weatherman, and he gave advice on where the toxic cloud might head. But most of all I broadcasted calls from frightened neighbors around the county. All night long, we comforted each other. It was one of the most rewarding events in the ten years I was a professional broadcaster. By morning all was safe.

I moved up the rungs of being an on-air personality and moved on to WIBM-FM 94 Gold and did my hit show 'Tom Patrick's Golden Overnights' in Jackson on a mid-Michigan 50,000 watt powerhouse. After I acclimated to a world where night is day and vice versa, I enjoyed the 11 pm to 6 am shift. I could play what I wanted and I actually developed a relationship with the overnight audience. I was #1 in my time slot, and I was making a little over the poverty level. Being on the radio was wonderful, but I never deluded myself into thinking I was actually in 'show business'. I've always said that I was just a guy spinning records and playing your favorite tunes. I was indeed 'town to town up and down the dial' and I think I moved 5 or 6 times in 2 years. I kept that U-Haul number on speed dial!

And then came radio automation and regulation… they didn't need DJ's let alone on-air personalities anymore. Show and song programming was now done by computer and even stop sets needed to be scripted. For me and millions of listeners the corporatization of radio killed everything we loved about it. Gone was the personality, spontaneity and creativity. And they did it many times as sneakily as possible. I was working at a radio station in central Florida. One day we saw 3-4 guys in suits descend upon the station and at the time did not think anything of it. That weekend during the overnight shift the station owner had quietly installed four reel-to-reel recorders behind a fake wall. Over the next week they recorded every Intro, Outro, time stop, PSA, News and station ID that went out over the air. The 'layoffs; began the following week and by the end of the month the

station was *entirely automated* with an air-staff gone from seven to one (the program director). Like Rock-n-roll itself, they squeezed out everything we loved about it in the name of profit and control. Personality radio was and is dead, and the shit we hear over the airwaves is now selected by corporate focus groups, record companies and ultimately, computers. They have made Radio into a robot with canned announcements and the same 40 songs over and over. It makes me want to puke.

I loved radio first and foremost because of the music and the ability to instantly connect with a listener. I'm fortunate that I love all kinds of music from Sinatra to Santana to Straight. But it was the connection with my listeners that was the real show with their crazy stories, locations and requests... that's what I miss the most. But it was not always fun and there were challenges. At one of my last stations I had a run in with the Station Manager almost to the point of violence... he and by extension the corporate office wanted to tell me not only what to play but what to *say* and it was not just for an air shift and a few commercials anymore now it was 24/7. The new memo said that any outside gig had to be OK'd by the Program Director and the station *always* got a cut... they called it an 'Appearance Fee'. So they basically owned my ass lock, stock and barrel and I did not like it. It came to a head and the Program Director, a sweet guy named Kemosabi Joe, could not save me from a vengeful and frankly short sighted Station Manager. I left shortly thereafter to pursue a show on Capitol Radio in London, England.

Radio is not a business to get rich in... semi-famous maybe, but not financially lucrative no matter what your ratings might be. You'll be loved by the community just not by your Banker. For example I was on the #1 morning show in the 11th largest radio market in America and I was making $38k a year. Sad. We got a nice fat bonus from corporate for our ratings, much to the chagrin of the Station Manager. But with the coming of pre-programmed corporate bullshit radio I saw the writing on the wall and it was time to hang up the old headphones and morph into something else, something new, something different... but what... or rather who?

I come from show biz... here's my Uncle Bill a broadway actor and dancer. He replaced Robert Preston in 'The Music Man' on Broadway. He also appeared on The Jackie Gleason Show (Left). My Aunt was a June Taylor Dancer on the show.

Far Left: Asst. Cruise Director Tom with Capt. Statius, SS Oceanbreeze

Below: I had the first Renault Le Car in the eastern US.

Chapter 7

Ladies and Gentleman...
Mr. Tom Patrick!
Becoming a Singing Comedian

*"I'm a born entertainer... When I open that fridge door
and the light goes on, I burst into song!"*
Robin Williams

They tell me, I always used to say... 'It's a nice night for
something...' and for me some of the sweetest and
scariest words I ever heard were (drum roll... announcer
voice...) "Ladies and Gentlemen Entertainer, Singer and
man about town...Tom Patrick!" Performing is both
scary and drug that keeps you coming back. I've always
been a natural entertainer, they tell me since the time I
could walk, and I think that's true... some people are just
born weird and are wired to be naturally funny.
Everybody thinks they have a sense of humor, about half
do, and those that can make others laugh are truly
special. I was, of course, always the class clown.

Even when I was in trouble, I could make light of the
situation, and even when others were angry with me, I
could lighten the mood. I've always been able to make
others laugh, and I consider it a blessing. My career in
show business started sort of behind the scenes as a DJ
for weddings and events, and then, of course, there was
Karaoke. When I lived there, San Francisco Weekly

Magazine called me "the King of San Francisco, Karaoke!" I did hundreds of gigs around the bay area and even performed at SF City Hall one time. I wound up being the Entertainment Director for Commodore Dining Cruises which was a Double Decked ship that served a high class dinner and entertainment on San Francisco Bay. I was the Host/MC and also performed Sinatra with backing track CDs in between the sets of the band. It was a wonderful time for me in the city by the bay with my new wife, Sharon. We had settled into a wonderful little flat so close to the Golden Gate Bridge we could hear the fog horns at night. We were very much in love. Still are.

I'd come home from the sea after working in the cruise ship business, but more on that in a minute... When I was working a Karaoke gig in downtown San Francisco I met a gentleman and was told about the San Francisco Comedy College. It's the same one that Robin Williams and Sinbad attended. The next day I went down and enrolled, and for the next 12 to 18 months, I worked on my 8 minutes; comedic timing, writing comedy bits, learning how to work the audience and learning how to promote. Every pro will tell you that the only way to get good is to get out there and be bad. I was well on my way up doing every open mic for 100 miles. After many sets that were bombs I started to get pretty good. I did some steady gigs but found out that I was basically a $100 a set guy. 'Tom's the Opener... not the Headliner!' It was a tough realization, but I thought, that's OK at least I was workin. However, I was a double threat because I could tell a good joke *and* I could sing a tune on key. And over the years, my singing voice has never failed me... I have tried to get rid of it but… Just kidding. But my efforts did lead to some successes. For example, I was the Finalist from the State of California and a top 10 finalist with singers from all 50 states for the 1998 National Karaoke Competition sponsored by Shure Audio Corporation. The finals were held in Laughlin Nevada, and Las Vegas. It was great to get stage time in a major venue before a large live audience.

Later, when I was an Assistant Cruise Director, I decided to migrate to being a full-time entertainer. Going from cruise staff to being a IRS1099 entertainer was difficult. I starved a lot, and I bombed a lot, but I was a modern-day Tommy Tumult! (A Tumult is a yiddish term for a guy that creates craziness and commotion in a crowd. Yep, that's me!) Helping audience members let their hair down or cruise ship passengers have the vacation of a lifetime was my goal. So lighten up and enjoy the craziness…I think the ship just docked at the wrong port!

In addition to being a performer, I wrote comedy for the one and only Kenny Smiles, a UK Blackpool Entertainer and Cruise Ship Headliner. He taught me how to be a Singing Comedian and in return I wrote bits and jokes for him. He passed in 2019. I was very lucky in entertainment pretty much for the rest of my life. I was the opening act for Capitol recording artist Laura 'Gloria' Branigan as well as the very popular Marilyn McCoo of the grammy award winning group 'The Fifth Dimension'. I once did a duet with her on the song 'Marry Me Bill'. Big time fun. They were both wonderful ladies, very gracious with a wonderful sense of humor.

But perhaps I'm getting a little bit ahead of myself. I was first contracted into the cruise line to be a cruise staff member and DJ with Ulysses LTD. They had two smaller, older, ships and it was a two-day trip to and from the Bahamas from Bayside in Miami. Then I became the DJ with Dolphin Cruise Lines. They also had two ships, the SS Sea Breeze and the SS Ocean Breeze doing eastern and western Caribbean runs. The eastern trip was to the Bahamas, Grand Cayman, Jamaica and sometimes Key West, while the western Caribbean run was to Grand Cayman, Jamaica and Cozumel Mexico and back. After being a DJ in the discotheque in the bowels of the ship, I

was promoted to being Stage Manager with a bump in pay came more responsibilities but it was exciting.

And it was really fortunate because I got an opportunity for almost a year to watch how world-class acts put it all together and produced it on a stage. I saw them backstage, I saw them during rehearsals, I saw how the songs were selected and how the different bits with audience interaction were scripted. It was a definite one-of-a-kind once-in-a-lifetime experience. By necessity I also became a pro with Sound and Lights. We dialed in the system and I had ship maintenance put a locked door on the audio cabinet and we had no problems after that.

After working for Dolphin Cruise Lines, I was recruited by Royal Caribbean Cruise Lines as a Assistant Cruise Director where I worked for a season but then the love of my life, Sharon and I decided to make a life together in San Francisco. I need to also mention that at the time, I did a wonderfully popular show called 'Salute to Sinatra' it was a 90 minute retrospective of Ol' Blue Eyes done to recorded big band tracks of the original Nelson Riddle arrangements. It became very popular. I had it charted out, but could never hire 12 to 15 musicians to do a full musical production. I had a lot of wonderful experiences while I was at sea in the cruise business but I believe the best thing was meeting my wife of now 30+ years, Sharon. She's my everything and more than I deserve.

Award winning Singing Comedian Kenny Smiles always use to tell me "other people are gonna believe about you what *you* believe about you!" The premise was the power of positive thinking… if you think you are gonna suck there's a 80% chance that you will <u>find</u> a way to make that happen. He also taught me to guard my personal time and privacy. I often wondered after I became friends with him, why he wasn't really a very social or 'party guy'

like his stage persona… he just wanted to chill out.
Maybe it was because he did nothing but please people
for 25 years; stood for ridiculous photographs, listened to
and positively responded to ridiculous comments, dealt
with musicians who were talentless or just plain lazy…
so when he was 'off' he just wanted to be left alone.
Thirty years on, I now understand. Most great comedians
are actually introverts at heart.

One of the men that has really made a difference in my
life is one of the funniest men I've ever met. Chris
Bockelman married my sister in college. He's a United
States Marine Corps veteran did a tour or two in Nam,
and he's a excellent singer and songwriter. He had a 1968
VW bug, and I remember one time after it snowed he
took me out for a ride and we went over by the school in
the parking lot, and he taught me about doing donuts and
about steering into the skid… And that's true about things
in life too… not just dealing with the dynamics of
steering a car you've got to steer into the skid sometimes
in life. Do what you fear most. Bockelman used to say
that I had the least amount of self-concern as anyone he
knew and I think know what he meant. I'm kind of like
the Italians, if you don't like me that's your problem not
mine. I never really cared too much about what others
thought about me but at the same time like anybody I
wanna be liked and I want to be popular. I don't need to
be right in most cases I know I'm right, so if other people
don't get that then that's something they have to deal
with not me. Life's too short to worry about gossip.
But the times have changed. There's a reason why the
comedian Dave Chapelle, and many other talents, no

longer do stand up… to him "we have become a nation of whiny little bitches" and audiences seem impossible to please, quick to anger, and slow to laugh. I have experienced this first hand; "Gee can you do something about the Sun?" "there's too much fooooood on this boat!" I swear there is a species of human being that is only happy when they're bitchin'. Many people will say that a lot of those people are from New York, and that is true, but New Yorkers are not rude–they're just direct, and that can be a good thing. If something sucks they will tell you. I received three standing ovations in my life and those were special, and I was honored but on the other side, I've also told a joke in front of 300 people and been met with complete silence. Now that's real horror!

So in one form or another, I've always been an entertainer, be it special events or clubs, bars, weddings and cruise lines along with a couple of contracts in Las Vegas for guys named Guido… I did anything to keep from getting a real job. I consider myself truly fortunate.

And be it playing in a rock band or acting in a film, doing a standup comedy or performing as a singing comedian, I found that on certain nights when the stars align and just the right audience is in the seats… I was able to create some truly memorable magic. And having the right audience in the right mood, makes all the difference. You cannot script spontaneity and that's where the true comedy comes from… not anything you can script. How are you gonna control the zombie idiot in the third row that you'll tease a little bit, make fun of, and help them and everyone have the time of their lives? I found it important that one makes fun of everyone.

One of the things they used to teach at San Francisco Comedy College and one of the things that gets new comedians into so much trouble is the concept of what they call "in the head out the mouth". You don't edit anything. Because those crazy comments from your subconscious are what can be truly funny. To laugh at our problems and to make fun of all equally was my hallmark. Sometimes during the show I didn't really have to do anything. It was the responses from the audience that you can't script that was truly hilarious. But its a dangerous tightrope that you can fall off of at any moment… ask Kramer from TVs 'Seinfeld'.

From Sinatra to Santana, and from Don Rickles to Robin Williams, I consider the moments I've spent on stage before an audience to be some of the best times of my life. Audience members who saw my shows would tell you that while I didn't always hit the mark comedically or musically I believe all of them would say that everyone always has a great time at a Tom Patrick show!

⊛

Chapter 8

Silly Con Valley
...Cause dat's where the money is!

"Silicon Valley is a mindset not a location!"
Reid Hoffman

So I had made my way to Northern California, where fortunes are made be it green gold in Humboldt County or digital gold in Silicon Valley. I call it Silly Con Valley because, many times, some of these companies are less than forthright with their end users, stockholders, or investors. Sharon and I got married and settled in to a working life in the city by the bay. I had been involved with the Amiga computer and and, peripherally the company of NewTek, which invented a thing called the

Video Toaster, which was basically a broadcast quality switcher, CG, Chron, Green screen system that produced NTSC broadcast quality video that you could put directly on the air. I was the Editor of Video Toaster User (VTU) and LightwavePRO Magazines (Lightwave was a 3D animation software). This was the bleeding edge of A/V technology, so once again, I was Forest Gump right on the edge, and this time it was for the digital media and streaming revolution.

When I was the Editor of VTU, I'll never forget when the representatives from a company called Micropolis came to our offices. They put a small case on the top of my desk, opened it, and inside was something that kind of looked like a small toaster. It was about maybe 10 inches long by 5 inches tall, white with a hard impact plastic cover, red access light and it was a five-gig hard drive. We all gathered around it like it was the holy grail, and we wondered how in the world we would ever fill up 5 Gigabytes of data. Little did we know that within a very short time storage devices with 100 times that in digital media storage space would be available.

The other thing I eventually learned was to always have a side gig. For example, I had a Mobile Video Production Company, and we would go and video company events, meetings, weddings etc., and stream it all out over the Internet. That, at the time, was a fairly major thing, but now is common place. I went to work for a European-based company. They had invented a similar device called 'The Video Machine' instead of being Amiga-based, it was more popular because it was PC/Windows-

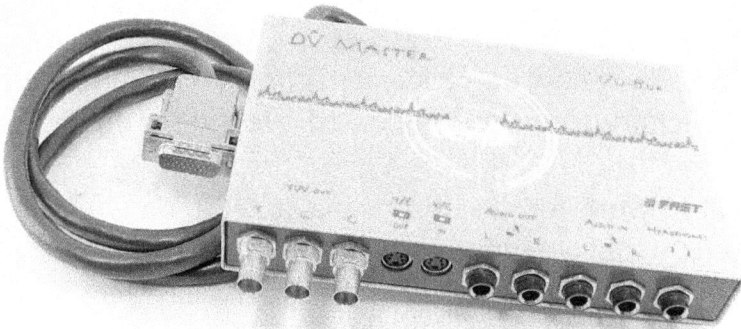

based, the company had approximately 25,000+ users even though their nonlinear post production system was fairly expensive at the time, costing around $8000 to $10,000 depending on how it was outfitted. But it could produce broadcast quality results, and if you went out and bought those same devices individually, you'd be talking of upwards of $30,000+. I was the company's Media Relations and Communications Director. I generated more media and press coverage than ever before including generating $2.3 million in editorial coverage in my first year alone. Because I had come from publishing, I was fairly good at getting coverage on our products and our people. This was the time that I basically broke the six-figure salary ceiling... I was making good money, my wife and I were healthy, happy and life was truly charmed.

I met a lot of incredible people working in Silicon Valley, one of which is a guy who is still a friend and partner today world-class artist and now college professor Gene Buban, he created the title cover of this book and some of my other books as well, he recently completed a huge art project for the California Department of Transportation and BART. He's now an Associate Professor at San Jose State University and is truly talented. He did the cover.

So I went to work for the Europeans, and after a while, it came to pass that a new product was to be introduced. Now, they always have plans. Short range plans like for the next 3 months and long range plans like five years out, and while they were concerned with quality, their main concern was numbers and profit like any good business. But they suffered from a lack of business decisiveness, and everything seemed to be done by committee. Nobody wanted to step out and make a decision or a statement, let alone solidify a product feature set. The fear of being wrong was pervasive.

I was one of the first in the entire western United States to have the new groundbreaking Sony DV Camera called the VX-1000. It was the first semi-pro camera that offered a 'Firewire' IEEE-1394 digital input/output so that you could shoot a video on DV tape and digitally transfer it to your laptop or computer for editing and post-production. At the time, it was pretty heady stuff, and I loved it. The CEO of the company, our lead software programmer, and, for some reason, myself were selected to go to Japan to talk with and possibly reach an agreement with Sony. We wanted them to provide us with CODEC chips that offer digital input/outfit and allow the encoding and decoding of a DV video signal in real time. Total digital quality end to end. It was supposed to work in real-time… it didn't (at least not with the speed of the computers available at the time). So, I made what I thought was the right decision, but in hindsight it wasn't.

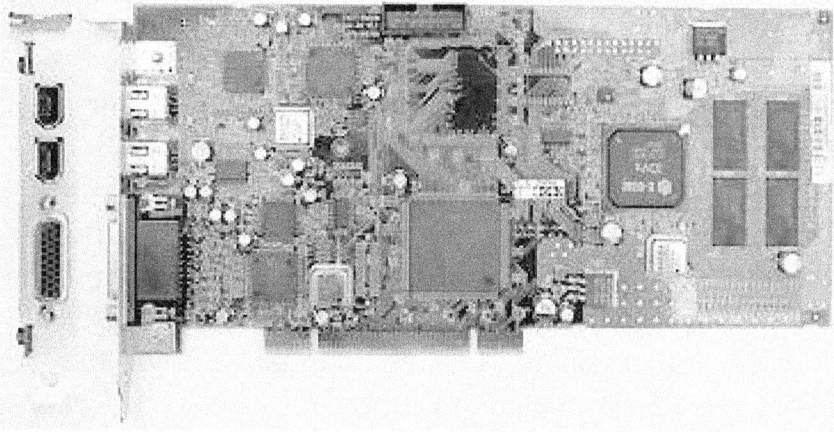

At the direction of the home office in Europe, my seniors in the company directed me to bury, deny, or best of all, not even acknowledge the fact that the product did not work as advertised. We knew that before we shipped more than 10,000+ units. And these were products that went for $1200-$1500. They were computer cards that you could slide into your PC and they had video inputs and outputs so you could use the computer as a video post-production center. The problem was not the hardware what we came to find is that it was the software and the fact that present-day computers were to slow to process a digital signal. Suffice to say without getting in the weeds... and it's probably too late for that... the product didn't work and I was forced to defend it in the press and with the end-user. I did so and I am ashamed to say that I had basically become a paid liar. Looking back now I can see that I had become addicted to the money. You know how it goes... you try to rationalize, you hear stories or you hear from end users... the ones who couldn't really afford a $1500 video paperweight and they had spent their last money to try and start a part-time video business to help their family get by. After a while, you can't even stand to look at the person in the mirror every morning. I had become addicted to the money.

One of the great things about working for this company was the opportunity once or twice a year to take trips to Europe. In the course of two or three years, I had visited the UK, France, Spain, Italy, and Germany. It was the third time I had traveled in Europe, the first when I was in the Navy, the second when I brought my Mom to Rome to see the Holy Father, and the third time was working for the Europeans. But all good things must come to an end, and I forget what the reason was, but the next thing I knew I saw the writing on the wall and decided to leave the company. About a year later the rumor was that the Feds... I think it was the Federal Trade Commission... was looking into irregularities in the company's financials and books.

After a while, the company decided to clean house, and they brought over a young 30-something to be CEO and run the company. He was I think the youngest CEO in the valley at the time and he was the epitome of the younger generation; laid-back but open to new ideas with a demand for innovation and results. A seriousness beyond his years with broad shoulders to carry his Germantic guilt. I remember one time he and I were driving to a meeting in his car, which naturally was a Mercedes, and the subject of World War II somehow came up.

Bob, like most Germans was a very upfront dude and he asked me, "Tom, do you blame me for what happened with the Nazi's and the Jews in World War II?" and he was very sincere. I thought about it for what seemed like two or three minutes, and I quietly responded, "Bob, I blame you for what happened with the Jews and the Nazi's in World War II like you should blame me for what happened to the blacks during the Civil War." It was obvious to me that even after all these decades, and even though he was of a totally different generation, the German psyche still has a good deal of guilt and sensitivity for what went on way back in the 'big one'.

While that was refreshing, there is no guilt in the Valley. The mentality is now one that says if you tell a big enough lie often enough, folks will eventually come to believe it as true. Its all about the Venture fund folks and the stockholders. Products that don't or barely work, non-existent tech support and feature sets that are more fantasy than fact… this is the Silicon Valley of today. But American consumers don't seem to care and the company's continue to make billions every year.

There's a reason why politicians come to Silicon Valley every election season to court the powers that be there and get donations… like Wille Sutton said… because that is where the money is. But we would do well to remember that it is a door that swings both ways… so when it comes to creating laws and regulations on the digital industry, legislators, be they in Sacramento or Washington DC, are sure to pick up the phone when the call comes in from the valley. It's all a con.

☙

Chapter 9

A POLITICAL MAVEN
The Art of Negotiation

"My choice early in life was between whether to be a piano player in a whorehouse or a politician… And to tell the truth, there's hardly any difference!"
President Harry S. Truman

I think former President Truman is right. I guess I got my interest in politics from my Mom. Doris used to say that 'all evil needs to triumph is for good men and women to sit around and do nothing!' Her political persuasion was kind of interesting; she was part libertarian, part Republican, and part Democrat. For example, she was sort of a John Bircher and fought for investigations into the water being chlorinated back in the early 60s. I remember vividly that she took me downtown to a public meeting and I think the city-county building inside a big auditorium where she and Jean Whelan, a family friend, stood up and questioned whether or not putting chlorine in the water was some sort of communist plot. I always thought my Mom would've made a good Senator. She always spoke her mind and believed in the little guy.

I've followed politics since the time I was in Saint Vincent's Children's Home in Lansing, Michigan, when I was able to go over to the state capital and watch the proceedings there. Fast forward 50+ years, and a few years ago, I ran a campaign for state senator in Florida by the first Latina to ever run for state-level office from our district. While we didn't win in a heavily red part of the state, we did garner more votes than any other Democratic candidate in the history of district elections. But I don't wanna get too far ahead of myself.

My first involvement in politics was when I helped to elect and re-elect Willie 'Mr. Slick' Brown to the California State Legislature. He eventually became Speaker and got a lot of things done for his constituents. I started as a volunteer and worked my way up to be a Precinct Captain in the San Francisco 16th precinct. And I learned how things were done. Speaker Brown had style; $1500 suits from Yves Saint Laurent, $1000 leather shoes from Italy. He showed me how to take care of constituents, whether it was just listening to a trivial complaint or making sure that thousands of dollars in frozen turkeys were distributed every holiday season. I basically was in charge of 'community outreach' and was a troubleshooter and overall facilitator. It was sometimes pretty boring work. One of the things I recall being responsible for was helping to secure voting locations where people could actually come and vote. Space in San Francisco is tight and sometimes it was actually just a persons garage! Not a great voting site, but you go to where it's convenient for the voters. The 16th precinct was heavily Asian and so having interpreters and ballots printed in various Asian languages was important. I learned a lot in those early days, but I didn't know at the time that the political skills I was learning would be of valuable assistance to me later in life.

Fast forward a lot of years, and my wife Sharon and I move from San Francisco to Oahu and I find that I am working at the Hawaii State Legislature in Honolulu. We lived on the windward side of the island and I enjoyed driving over the Pali Mountain every day to the capitol. While working there first I worked for the Democratic Party, and then I worked for a major Democratic State Representative, representing the Big Island. Now, Hawaii ever since it became a state in 1959, the state has always been held by the Democrats almost to the detriment of things. When I was there, only one Republican was in office. I believe in political balance, and I also like a good fight, so in Hawaii, I basically joined the Republicans, or at least the Libertarian Party. I believed the government at both the state and Federal levels had gotten out of control and needed to be cut down to size. I was young and naïve.

I was a speaker at one of the very first Tea Party protests in the USA which was held on the steps of the Hawaii state capitol with 5000 attending. I didn't speak long...

"I thought you all should see what a blue Dog Democrat looks like!" I said. (a Blue Dog Democrat is...) "A fiscally conservative social liberal, strong on national defense and steadfast in protecting liberty. To the powers that be I say... It is our money and we have a right to see how you are spending it... Thank You!"

I took 2 minutes as opposed to the other speakers who said the same thing in 20. The crowed seemed to appreciate the brevity. It was one of the largest political gatherings in state history.

My time working at the state house was challenging but rewarding. I made it a point to learn all about the building and the grounds which were right next to the palace of the Hawaiian Kingdom. The Capitol, built in 1969, is a fascinating building, and if you're ever in Honolulu, I highly suggest a visit. It's filled with stories. For example, one of the early Governors, Bill Quinn, who began his Governorship in 1959 when Hawaii became a state, used to love smoking cigars. He would come out on the balcony outside the Governor's office and smoke a cigar. He successfully served the state and eventually passed away. About a week later, the night

watchman reported, and for several other times over the years, on certain nights, if you look up from the ground

floor up to the balcony outside the governors office, you
can sometimes see a small wisp of white cigar smoke.

Now, I need to say something that's not gonna be very
popular with some folks, I found Hawaii to be one of the
most racist places on the planet. If you were a hoale (a
white person) with blonde hair and blue eyes for the most
part, you're going to have a problem in the islands. Even
if you are of the Aina. Yet somebody from the Philippines
with black hair and brown eyes is considered to be a local
from day one. I had many animated discussions about
this issue… they kept asking for their stolen land and I
told him my portion was in the trunk of the car, and
they're welcome to it! I'll put it bluntly they don't like
white people there. And maybe I don't blame them. If I
was born and raised in a place and couldn't afford a place

to live, I think I would be upset too. Locals have been priced out of their own neighborhoods. But you either believe that all men are created equal, or you don't. And that is part of the problem I have with all of the monarchies… to say that one person is better than another because of the blood that runs through their veins is, I feel, the very antithesis of what America is all about. Royalty is an old and quaint idea whose time has passed.

One thing that's not talked about very often for fear of scaring tourists is that there's a growing and loud call for Hawaiian independence. Sometimes, I think this might not be a bad idea when one looks at the amount of federal dollars that flow to Hawaii. Financially speaking the United States, may be better off with Hawaii as its own country. We'll keep Pearl Harbor as it has been purchased in blood. Some there think old whitey is all evil, they should try and run a state as large and diverse as Hawaii. Sadly, unqualified candidates have been given preferential treatment based on skin color and locale, and they pretty much pull all the local strings… as I write this, we saw how that worked with the fires on Maui.

Working at the Capitol, my Representative's office had a balcony that overlooked the Iolani Palace grounds next door. Built in 1879, the palace is absolutely gorgeous. Its 10 acres are surrounded by a stone and iron fence with gates so the grounds can be secured. Visitors can go and have a picnic on the lawn or take a tour, and it truly is worth an afternoon. One day, I was out on the balcony eating my plate lunch. I looked over and saw two men with dark sunglasses standing by the palace gate, and I thought it looked rather odd like they were two FBI agents or something. Certainly it looked out of place.

After I finished my plate lunch of Kalua Pork, Cabbage, and Rice I started to make my way to the Post Office which is on the far side of the palace grounds. I would always walk through the gate and walk through the palace grounds to the other side and back as a sort of shortcut. By the time I got to the gate, the two large Hawaiian men with dark sunglasses had chained the gate shut and were standing directly in front of the gate. When I asked why I could not pass, they said that the palace had been "re-occupied by the sovereign nation of Hawaii." I told them in no uncertain terms that there was no such thing and that very respectfully, the powers to be in law enforcement were going to be on their way. I went back to the office. I did exactly that. I called the United States Park Service, the local Honolulu Police, the Capital Police, and the FBI...

Over the next three days, the palace grounds were occupied by two dozen Hawaiian independence activists. Every day, the chief of police and they would talk story on a large blanket underneath the Banyan tree "negotiating." Word of the takeover of the palace reached Washington DC and received state-wide and national news coverage. It brought the Hawaiian Independence movement more credit and acknowledgment than it deserves at least in my opinion. No sooner had they come then 3 days later, they simply left. No explanation, no press event, they simply disappeared. And to this day they've been mostly silent.

One of the most outspoken experts about the lack of legitimacy in the claims by the Hawaiian sovereignty movement is Dr. Ken Burgess and after rumors of paramilitary training by independence activists going on in the hills above Waianae on Oahu, including firearms training, it was decided by many of us that a peace conference would be a good thing. Nothing formal, just a chance to sit down in a circle and 'talk story' about each other's points of view. I've always thought talking is a good thing and I was honored to help organize the first native Hawaiian Independence-State of Hawaii peace conference. In addition to Bumpy Kanahele from the re-established Hawaiian nation there were other Native Hawaiian leaders. In addition, anti-independence author Dr. Ken Burgess and Dick Roland, President of the Grassroots Institute, were there as were two state senators. We spent nearly 2 hours exchanging views, eating poi, and trying to create a sense of Ohana (family). And while it was not a complete failure it was less than fully successful and no further talks were held to my knowledge. Still I am proud to have played a small part in addressing and exploring the issue.

I had become fairly vocal about my opposition to Hawaiian Independence. This made me a friend of some but an enemy to most, so at the end of the legislative session, it was mutually decided that I leave the Hawaii state legislature. A very nice lucrative position was created for me at The Grassroot Institute of Hawaii. It is basically a libertarian think tank that generates research and does advocacy in the community for libertarian and frankly conservative causes. It's funded by the Koch

Brothers, Americans for Prosperity, and Grover Norquist' 'Americans for Tax Reform'. I was there, when, during a speaking engagement, Norquist said he didn't want to kill government... He just wanted to make it small enough so he could drag it into the bathroom and drown it in the bathtub! It was a comment that received wide press coverage across the country.

The Grassroot Institute was part of an organization called The State Policy Network. This shadowy organization established a plan to establish 'think tanks' in every state. Funded by tobacco, casino and anti-abortion money, they came up with a 10-year action plan 5 years ago...

1) Pack the Courts with conservative Judges - *Done*

2) Overturn Roe v. Wade - *Done*

3) End affirmative action

4) Deny climate change and any government-based solution to address same. And, more importantly, *sow misinformation* about the global warming. - *Done*

5) Establish 'Think Tanks' to push conservative issues and legislation in every state. - *Done*

The State Policy Network has been extremely successful implementing their agenda in a very short time. For example, on Oahu, they have stalled and been against rail transportation from day one. Why is beyond anyone's guess except perhaps the automobile and gas interests. Anyone who has tried to drive the H1 freeway on Oahu in Honolulu between 7 AM and 7 PM will know that rail is desperately needed. H1 is a parking lot that crawls at 20 miles an hour all day long.

The Institute hired former Miss Texas, and a Miss America top-10 runner-up to lead the organization's efforts. She was everything that you would expect in a beauty queen... beautiful, fairly articulate but a political lightweight... she was also devious and less than honest. I was being paid a great salary, like when I was a PR Manager in Silicon Valley, and I was forced to publicly take positions on and even testify on issues that I totally disagreed with. It was what I was paid for but I started to quietly plan a strategic exit. I went on my first vacation in 3 years, and when I returned two weeks later, I saw the writing on the wall and knew it would be a month, if that. I began to plan my exit. Not easy in a limited job market.

Actually, my leaving had been building for quite some time, but I think the straw that broke, the camel's back in my case, was when they sponsored a Climate Change Conference in Honolulu with known global warming

deniers. I advised against it, and it did damage the Institute's credibility. I mean, these guys were full fraudsters with fake research and academic papers that weren't peer-reviewed running around making wild assertions. They are basically saying that we should do nothing and that it is all a liberal conspiracy. The fact that the highest temperatures in recorded history are occurring as I write this with more and more natural disasters due to carbon use… we should just ignore all that because it's all part of 'God's plan'. What misguided hubris!

I'm never one to take information blindly, I think that's what makes me a good writer and a good journalist, so I went with my wife and my mother-in-law to Alaska and we saw first-hand the glaciers and how they used to be 20 miles that way and are now another 30 miles inland. I saw upfront how the ice is melting more rapidly. It's obvious to me that whether it's natural or man-made, something's happening, and it's a problem. Like a frog in

Tom McAuliffe

DIRECTOR OF COMMUNICATIONS

1314 S. King Street, Suite 1163
Honolulu, Hawaii 96814

808 591 9193

808 356 1690

808 282 8478

tom@grassrootinstitute.org

grassrootinstitute.org

GRASSroot
Institute of Hawaii

a pot of slowly boiling water, we seem to be either too blind or too stupid to do anything to save ourselves.

It was time to move on. I never truly felt comfortable in the islands, and as beautiful as it was we found that in order to live there, we had to work all the time so we didn't really have time to go and truly enjoy the beauty and splendor. For example, in the six or seven years I lived there I think I only went SCUBA diving twice and snorkeling a dozen times, but that said? Waking up and looking at the green Ko'olau Mountains on the windward side of Oahu every morning was truly inspirational.

In Hawaii, we were poor, so once an offer came to move back to the mainland we jumped at the chance. And to show you how God blesses those who honor him… you'll never guess where it was that we received an offer of employment from a mainland resort company in, that's right, one of my favorite places on the planet, the Emerald Coast between Pensacola and Panama City on the still gorgeous Gulf of Mexico.
The local resort rental company had seen my wife's Sharon's online work and tendered an offer, which she accepted. She was on the ground floor of the digital

reservations revolution in hotel and resort e-commerce so the Florida company recruited her and moved us from Hawaii to Florida in about 8 to 10 weeks. In Hawaii, our funds were stretched and limited, but in Florida, we're much better off because there's no state tax, and the cost-of-living is much lower. We were able to realize our dream of having a waterfront home and a boat. We even had our own dock on the Intercoastal Waterway! It was redneck heaven, but I had to find a job, and when that proved to be too difficult, I fell back on the only thing I really knew and that was media, music and entertainment. It was to be a tough nut to crack.

I established one of the most popular and award-winning music duos on the Gulf Coast, 'Latitudes' played it all from the Beatles to Tony Bennett. We were a 3 time Beachcomber Music Awards nominee. For the next 4-5 years, we played every dive from the Florida Bama state line to the beaches of 30a and Panama City. It's was fun but grueling work and did not pay well although we always drank and ate for free. Eventually, I could not deal with the heat, moving heavy equipment, and the growingly rude clientele. Perhaps more importantly, my duo partner had a heart attack and died. Very sad. We made some truly beautiful music together and our CD 'Europa' is still popular and selling. I will occasionally do gigs for charity, but pretty much I've been concentrating on songwriting and writing books.

Over the years, from the time of the antiwar protests in Detroit and the University of Michigan in Ann Arbor to even today, although less so, I've always been impressed with the power of music to sway attitudes and public opinion. I would submit that it was protest music that helped to end the Viet Nam war.

Things have changed a lot since then, and these days I believe in the 'no incumbent' party! I believe that the founding fathers never intended public service to be a profession... you were supposed to go and serve your fellow citizens and then go back to being a blacksmith, rancher, farmer, whatever. Now we've got guys who have been in 'public service' for more than 40 years now. Enough! If you've been up there in DC for more than two terms, you better sharpen up your résumé because you are going out. Frankly, we need good people like YOU to run! And whether you're Democrat or Republican or Independent, I believe the system only works if we work it. Together, I still believe we can reach a consensus and move the people's train down the tracks. Leave your rancor and talkin' about my mama at the door, and let's roll up our sleeves to help America fulfill its full promise.

I won't go into politics at length suffice to say that there's enough blame to go around. We voted for Obama because we wanted change... Nothing did. We got so pissed off we voted for Trump cause we wanted change... nada changed. We found out that it's the same thief... just a different set of clothes! When I read books by John Adams and the other founding fathers, it's very obvious to me what they intended and this ain't it! We now have people who've been up there on capitol hill for 40+ years... they've never had a regular job. And to them I say, sharpen up your resumes because you're going out the door! We want term limits, and we want to rescind

Citizens United. Our Constitution does not say that a company should have the same rights as a citizen and we must get the money out of politics. Join the 'no-incumbent' party today! Two terms and out.

One thing is certain… if we as citizens don't get involved… anything can happen–and it probably will!

⊛

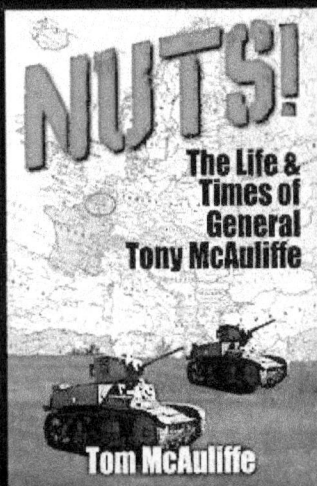

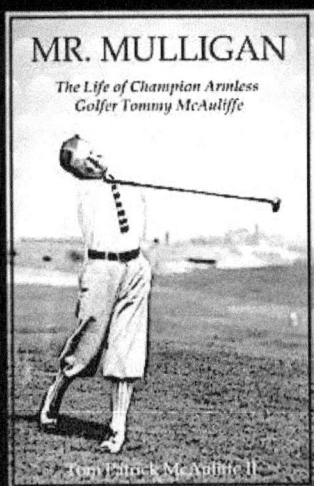

Chapter 10

Author, Author!
The Life of a Ink Slinger

*"A writer is not a confectioner, a cosmetic dealer,
or an entertainer."*
Anton Chekhov

I've always admired engineers of the written word. From
as far back as when I was in high school, I have always
had a gift for communicating. In the Navy, as a
Photojournalist, I was working for All Hands and
Campus Magazines, and I was able to put a few
sentences together while entertaining and educating my
readers.

Later, as Editor at Video Toaster User magazine then as
West Coast Editor of Singer Magazine and Contributing
Editor at Digital Content Producer Magazine, and later
Editor in Chief of Government Video Magazine…
publishing came to be in my blood. I liked the challenge
of doing a totally new issue every month. It's safe to say
I've been around the pen and typewriter for more years
than I care to admit. Publishing is a cutthroat business
with plagiarists and opportunists around every corner.
Artificial Intelligence will also prove to be a double-edge
sword. And we must come to grips with how AI content
is to be used. These days truth seems to be an
afterthought, or merely a passing consideration. "If it
doesn't cost us anything, sure we'll be honest." I'll never

TEACHER ASTRONAUT CHRISTA MCAULIFFE

Written & Narrated by
Tom McAuliffe

THROTTLE UP!

Book #3:
The McAuliffe Files

forget when I was talking with my publisher, and this is a magazine with a circulation of about 100,000, so it is no small fry and I said. 'well, naturally, I understand it's all about circulation…' To which he responded, "No, Tom, it's about our *advertisers*." And in the niche of magazines covering audio and video production where the subscriptions are free, he was exactly right. Never bite the hand that feeds you!

And as much as I love the digital world and the wonderful things that online content allows us to enjoy and partake in, for us old schoolers, there's nothing like the look, and feel of an artistically laid out and slickly produced magazine. Besides, you really can't or shouldn't take your laptop into the toilet with you and you can do that all day long with a magazine. For me, a hard copy of the printed medium is the only way to go.

I've hit the big 65 now. I'm retired and plan on finishing my life sharing wonderful stories that need to be told. When it comes to independent publishing, I have good news and bad news... The good news is now anyone can produce a high-quality bookshelf ready book, eBook or Audiobook. The bad news? Anybody can now produce a book, eBook or Audiobook! Consequently, there's a lot of term paper quality books on the market that in my opinion, don't deserve a readers money and more importantly a readers time. If you wouldn't mind I would greatly appreciate a honest review or feedback.

The recent motion picture 'Hidden Figure's' about the black women scientists at NASA really opened my eyes. I've been a NASA follower and supporter since I was eight years old watching Alan Shepard in orbit. The film and the contribution from these ladies of color made quite an impression on me. I said to myself, 'I wonder how many other inspirational, historical stories are out there that have been suppressed or ignored, that we don't know about?' I believe there are lots of stories like that. I'm working on a few of them right now! These are almost unbelievable and undiscovered real-life stories that deserve to be told. Telling stories that will have an impact upon one's life is always my goal. Let it be the truth or not at all. Most folks die with stories still inside them... I'm bound and determined that not happen to me. I've written five books in 2 years and thanks to you I've won seven book awards so far with thousands of volumes sold. I hope you will check out my books if possible!

•Mr. Mulligan - T*he Life of Champion Armless Golfer Tommy McAuliffe*
The story of my grandfather, who lost both arms in a streetcar accident when he was eight years old and taught himself how to play par golf. He played with golf greats like Arnold Palmer, Bobby Jones, and Walter Hagen, and traveling the world, teaching others about the power of positive thinking.

•Nuts! *The Life and Times of General Tony McAuliffe*
Working with the General's last living relative, we uncover the true story of the legend of General Mac courageously saying 'Nuts!' to the Germans, when surrounded in the city of Bastonge during World War II's Battle of the Bulge.

•Throttle up! *Teacher Astronaut Christa McAuliffe*
The life of famous teacher, and want to be astronaut, her teaching philosophy and her experience being the first civilian in space. We examine her tragic death in the Space Shuttle Challenger because of political go fever, and negligence on the part of NASA and the Reagan administration is also covered.

•Mad Dog -*Detroit Tiger, Dick McAuliffe*
The career of major league, baseball player, Dick McAuliffe, who proved that attitude and hustle on the baseball field, were as important as sheer stats.

•Almost –*the Road to the Grande*

Detroit rock bands that were local stars but never made it nationally, bands like The Rationals, Frost, Savage Grace, SRC, the Gang, the Pyramids, Band X, and so many others. And how these virtually unknown local bands influenced the soon to be famous bands from the UK like; Led Zeppelin, The Who, Cream, The Faces, Rod Stewart, Jeff Beck and soooooo many major rock acts. Since 1928 the Grande was one of the best ballrooms in America!

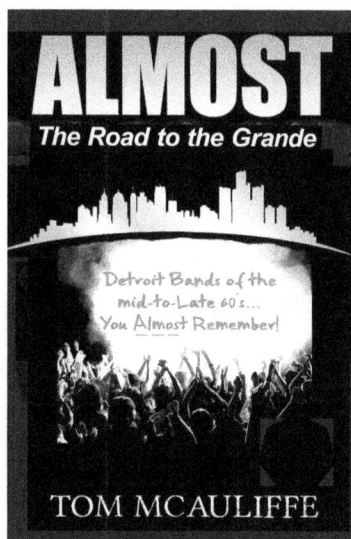

And lastly, the book that is in your hands… my memoir 'Charmed'. I know it can seem too incredible to be believed… looking back, sometimes I don't even believe it myself, but every single word is true. I hope you've had or will have as fulfilling, interesting and intense a life as I have. From my time in Motown to the US Navy's Combat Camera Group, I've been truly blessed. THANK YOU for your support!

Chapter 11

Florida: God's Waiting Room
Roasting in the Sunshine

"In Florida, we salt Margaritas, not sidewalks!"
Unknown

It all goes around in circles, and I find myself back where it almost all began and certainly where I became a young man. I am back in the land of the blue hair and red neck. The Florida Emerald Coast is just this side of heaven. It is rather undeveloped, because for years there was a "not in my backyard" mentality, and developers were kept at bay. That's not true anymore, and there are sadly few places where one can still experience 'old Florida'. They say that you can never go home again. I'm not so sure that's true because it certainly felt like I was coming home. It's the Redneck Riviera, and the culture is one of God, Guns, and the great outdoors. Fishing, hiking, swimming, and snorkeling are the pastimes of the Sunshine State. The Panhandle is politically very red.

But the main reason I moved from paradise in Hawaii 5000 miles to Florida was to try and have a relationship with my family again. That was one of the main reasons. While it might not be the paradise that Hawaii is, Florida is certainly the next best thing. They say that God moves in mysterious ways and that's certainly true in my life because six months after we closed on our dream home, the worlds largest and worse oil spill in history occurred approximately 237 miles away from our new home. Ahhh the luck of the Irish!

The BP Horizon oil spill in 2010 decimated the Gulf and certainly the resort and hospitality communities. We had just moved from Hawaii and Sharon spent two months doing things like shooting video of the beaches showing people that there were no oil slicks. As bad as the oil spill was westward in Louisiana, Mississippi and Alabama in Florida the beaches were relatively unaffected. There were some tarballs, but all in all the Florida beaches were fine. But despite a valiant effort by local media, resort and hotels business basically stopped and the layoffs were massive. The effect on the local economy was devastating and is still being felt.

The damage that the Deep Water Horizon and BP caused will be felt for generations. One thing that nobody talks about is the fact that there is now a dead zone in the Gulf mainly caused by the chemicals used to dispersed the oil... some say the patch could be as long as 150 miles x 50 miles. Visiting the affected areas over in Mississippi and trying to do some community assistance work and seeing affected animals is enough to break your heart. I'm all for energy independence, but I don't think we should be drilling

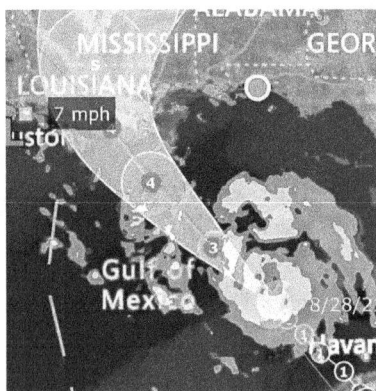

on the moon... And that's what the equivalent is to how deep they were and are drilling even today. You might as will be drilling on the dark-side of the Moon! You're working at depths where the pressure and the variables are almost unknown. One mistake equals catastrophe!

One also notices that it keeps getting hotter, and we now have problems like toxic algae... Algae so toxic that it'll peel the paint off of multi-million dollar fiberglass yachts. And the general consensus seems to be "if it doesn't affect me directly I don't really care" and another notion I dislike is; "God gave the earth to man to use as man sees fit!" Talk about shortsightedness! But let's be clear, with the way the glaciers are melting Florida, or at least a vast portion of it, will soon be underwater. The springs and water table has already started to disintegrate and be infiltrated by salt water add to that major bottlers using Florida springs to bottled water for sale, and it's easy to see the states days may be numbered. It won't happen in my lifetime, but certainly in your grandchild's lifetime. And let's be clear as the seas rise certainly America will protect places like Manhattan, Norfolk, and Washington DC from rising waters, but let's be honest, sadly, the birthplace of jazz, New Orleans, as well as Key West, will be condemned to King Neptune's depths and the sea. Sad. Its gonna happen, even DOD thinks so.

So here I am 65 years on from those streets of Detroit I so love, with my beautiful wife, my furry Cats, in a community that we love... But you know it's funny, I look at the face in the mirror, and sometimes it feels like I'm somebody else. Inside I don't feel like I'm 65... I still feel like I'm 35. Sadly after I cut the lawn or go snorkeling, I know what my age really is. They say that your senior years are your 'golden years'… We shall see. But from having to pee every five minutes to only having semi-annual erections to every single bone in my body hurting… we're off to a wonderful start.

⊛

Chapter 12

20-20 Hindsight
Looking Back, Looking Forward

"Dying is easy... Comedy is hard!"
Peter O'Toole as 1950s Movie Star Alan Swan

Looking back is always beneficial if done in moderation.
As we've discussed I guess my family is fairly normal
because it is highly dysfunctional. Although my returning
from Hawaii to try and reestablish a relationship with my
family was semi-unsuccessful. Looking back I realized it
was my fault because I was the one that left and was
away for
so many
years
following
my
dreams. I
still love
each and
every one
of them,
but
there's
nothing
you can
do if they
don't love

you back. Fights over politics, how my Mom was treated at the end of her life, and fights about money have destroyed our family. It's just my personal opinion, but I think my Mom would be very displeased. But I like to think that the lines of communication between us are just temporarily disconnected not permanently.

You can love your family and not like them very much, which I'm sure they would no doubt agree with. As the song goes 'Regrets, I've got a few', but I continue to hope and, where possible, try. And I want to be clear that over my life I have learned a lot from my siblings.

From my sister Elaine... I learned style and class.

From my brother Matt… I learned hustle and persistence.

From my sister Diane… I learned compassion and forgiveness.

Let me take this opportunity to thank each of them. They are each wonderful people in their own right, and while we don't speak regularly, I think of them fondly and often. You need to Treasure your family… it's the only one you're ever gonna get.

It took me 40-plus years and the help of a truly great woman, to learn that it really is all about love. One of God's true angels on earth, Sharon Louise Harvill McAuliffe, changed my life and, like it says in the movie, 'you make me want to be a better man'. She is the love of my life, my best friend, and an awesome business partner. Sharon, I love you.

You must admit our love-story is a unique one. I met her on a cruise and we had a bi-coastal love affair. She took a chance on me and is a truly loving and intelligent woman. We got married under the snowy pines of Lake Tahoe and have been together for more than 30 years. We have built a fulfilling and successful life together through hard work and good luck. And by giving each other the room to grow and be our own persons.

So here we are. I'm not really famous, I'm not really rich, and I'd like to tell you that there's some great and profound wisdom I've found on top of a mountain somewhere. Sorry. The true life lessons I've learned have always been simple but uncompromising. Maybe sometimes things are so simple we can't even see them. So that your time will be well spent please let me leave you with some tips and advice.

I hope that all this helps you lead a better life. I am a happy graduate of the school of hard knocks, and I have an advanced degree in failure as much as success. May yours be as interesting!

From my time growing up in the Motor City to the stage to Combat Camera Group, it's been phenomenal. I think when I get to the gates they'll say; "Well done, and welcome home." Thru the tears, laughter, disappointments and victories it's been a remarkable journey and I have indeed been fortunate. I wish you my kind of success and I wish you a fulfilling and 'charmed' life.

Tom's Top 10 Life Lessons

10) Treat others as you want to be treated.

9) Take care of your body and mind.

8) Read!

7) Look after your money.

6) Be it skydiving or starting a new business, don't be afraid to take chances.

5) When someone shows you who they are… believe them.

4) Fuck me once, shame on you, fuck me twice, shame on <u>me</u>.

3) Life is short; have fun!

2) Dance like nobody is watching and sing like nobody's listening.

1) Love with all your heart.

MORE MUSIC FOR YOUR HEAD !

Scarlet Omen
Kick = Ass = Rock & Roll

MARK • 349-3861   TOM • 474-8074

PICTURES & CLIPS

ncert in Navarre, FL

Cruise ship duo with Yuki from Japan

The Aqua Band, Oahu, Hawaii

Latitudes Duo with Guitarist Joe Klir

DETROIT, MICHIGAN - THE CITY OF THE STRAITS

The two Bobalo Boats provided tons of gigs to local bands with two dance floors.

Right:
Bahamas Film Shoot

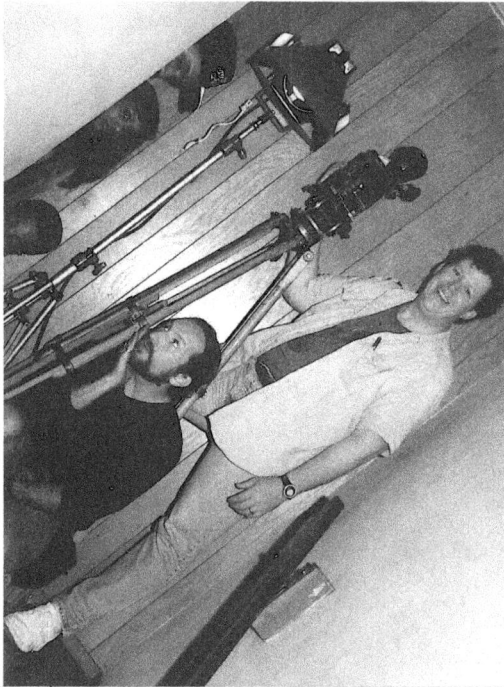

Below: Handmade
Gig Flyer

LETTERS TO THE EDITOR

Tune in to Civics 101

I would like to commend the City of Fort Walton Beach and Cox Cable for broadcasting City Council meetings on Community TV Channel 6.

It really helps track important issues and keep and eye on our public servants. Now all we need is some more community access video programs giving citizens an even bigger and better voice on local television and we'll be all set!

In many communities, as part of the franchises agreement, the cable company agrees to provide a small TV studio for citizens like you and me to create and record programs about local issues and interests.

Take a look at Crestview Community TV for how it is done. They consistently keep the folks in the north end of the country informed and on primary election night CCTV were the only ones doing live election results coverage ... and doing it very well indeed.

They say that an informed voter is a better voter, so let's hope that a more encompassing "FWB Citizens TV" channel is in our near future.

Tom McAuliffe, Fort Walton Beach

Top Left: Tom as Santa, SS Seabreeze

Center Left: Headliner Tom

Bottom Left: Latitudes Duo

Right: Reggae Tom

Left: *Tommy McAuliffe exhibit Kissimmee CC*

Below: *Tom lower left with* legs crossed

Bottom: *PADI Adv. Diver*

History in Print

Exciting Real-Life Stories from Local Author

Local award-winning Author Tom Patrick McAuliffe of Fort Walton Beach has been a busy writer of late! He has not one but two new books out now: *Mr. Mulligan—The Life of Champion Armless Golfer Tommy McAuliffe* and his latest effort, *NUTS! The Life and Times of General Tony McAuliffe*. Both titles are available as Paperbacks, eBooks and Audiobooks at Amazon, Kindle, Apple Books and at the local FWB Books-A-Million bookstore.

"*Mr. Mulligan* is about my Grandfather who lost both arms in a tragic street car accident at age nine, yet taught himself how to play PAR golf and lead a successful life. He played with Golf greats like Walter Hagen, Bobby Jones and Arnold Palmer. In the 1930s, the elder McAuliffe traveled the country as a Vaudeville entertainer and later was involved with helping to pass legislation to protect the rights of the handicapped," said Tom. "In the 40s and 50's, he would travel of the country and give positive thinking talks about overcoming life's obstacles. His motto was, 'The only handicap in life is a mental one! The armless Golfer was featured in newspapers, on TV, on radio and in 'Ripley's Believe it or Not' where he was featured twice, once in 1956 and again in 2013. Tom has also edited and published a companion volume called 'No Handicaps' which was first written by his

Grandpa Tommy in 1939—more than 25,000 words via a pencil in his mouth and one typewriter key at a time!

The second new title has just been published and *Nuts! The Life of General Tony McAuliffe* is now available. It chronicles the life of one of the U.S. Army's most colorful Generals from WWII documenting the Battle of the Bulge, the true version of the 'Nuts' message to the German's demanding our surrender at Bastogne and the General's 33+ year career defending America. "We would all be speaking German now if it wasn't for the brave men and women of 'The Greatest Generation,'" Tom said.

Tom, 65, lives in Elliot's Pointe with his realtor wife, Sharon, and cat, Gigi, and loves his new home town. "Moving from Hawaii almost 10 years ago, we found another kind of paradise in Fort Walton Beach and from the local culture to the beach, we love it here!" he said. He's a former Photojournalist with the U.S. Navy's Combat Camera Group and a graduate of the DOD's Mass Communications Program at Syracuse University. He is also a former magazine editor and writer with more than 25 years of bylines.

"I truly love writing and have always been an ol' Irish story teller," he said. "In these crazy times, there's nothing better than sitting down with a good Book, eBook or Audiobook!"

Tom has three more books planned for this year-one on teacher McAuliffe called Throttle Up!, another on MLB World Champion baseball player Dick McAuliffe called Mad Dog; and a final title in the five book McAuliffe Series. "Book 5 is about my cousin, former Virginia Governor and possible presidential candidate, Terry McAuliffe, called Life of the Party," said Tom. "All of the McAuliffe clan is related and traces its roots back to County Cork, Ireland in 1600," he said. "What a crazy family, eh?" Tom will be the featured author at the FWB Library Open House on Oct. 10th from 4-7 p.m. For more information, visit: www.authortommcauliffe.com.

Top: Fiji Islands
Left: Asst. Cruise Director
Bottom left: Showbill
Bottom Right: Taiwan

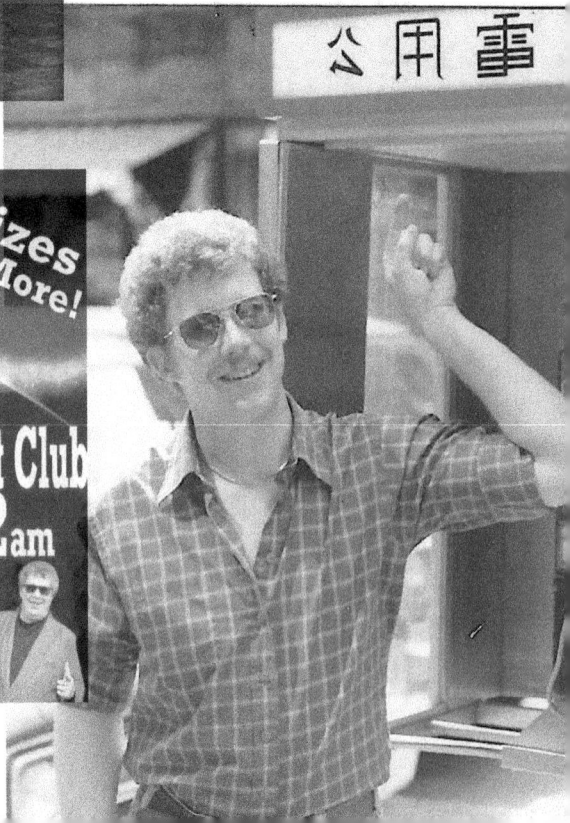

*Right: Friend &
Actor Dick Van
Dyke, 1989*

*Center: Lead
Singer, 1979*

Below: Show bills

A Night of Music and Comedy
With Singing Comedian
TOM PATRICK
And Special Guests!

LIVE!

CLUB 101
at *The Englander*
101 Parrott ~ San Leandro

Classic Rock &
Swing Music Dancing
with Clean Comedy
Great Brews & Food!

**THURSDAYS
7-11pm**
Cover Only $5 • Reservations Accepted

Info & Res. @ **510.357.3571**
www.tompatrick.com

**LAS VEGAS
NIGHTS** Starts 7/17!

A Night of Music, Comedy and Magic
www.laqsvegasnightsshow.com

LIVE! at *The Englander*

Starring: Singing Comedian
TOM PATRICK
Show $15   Hypnotist
Dinner & Show   **DAVE HILL**
Special Only $30!   Singer
LYNDA NOBLE

See Your Server for Tickets!
THURSDAY 8 PM

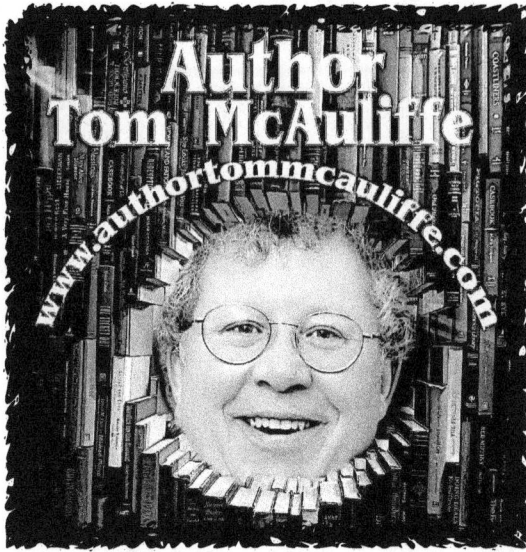

Author
Tom McAuliffe
www.authortommcauliffe.com

Please visit:

www.authortommcauliffe.com

Please leave us a review!

100% HUMAN CREATED CONTENT

<u>Acknowledgments</u>

The Sharon Harvill Foundation
The McAuliffe Heritage Center, Ireland
Diane & Chris Bockelman
Eve Ifft
The Detroit News
Dolphin Cruise Lines
Royal Caribbean Cruise Lines
US Navy Public Affairs
Draft 2 Digital
CREEM Magazine
FWB Life
The San Francisco Comedy College

<u>*Special Thanks to:*</u>

Dale L Roberts
Editor Jan Brown
Dick Van Dyke
Pete 'Grack' Washburn
Artist Gene Buban
Tom Hawkinson
Dave Lehto
Joe Kline
Kenny Smiles
Kim Ball
Jerry Brazil
Cece Gables
Brittney Bockelman
Sam the Photoshop God

Tom's Books

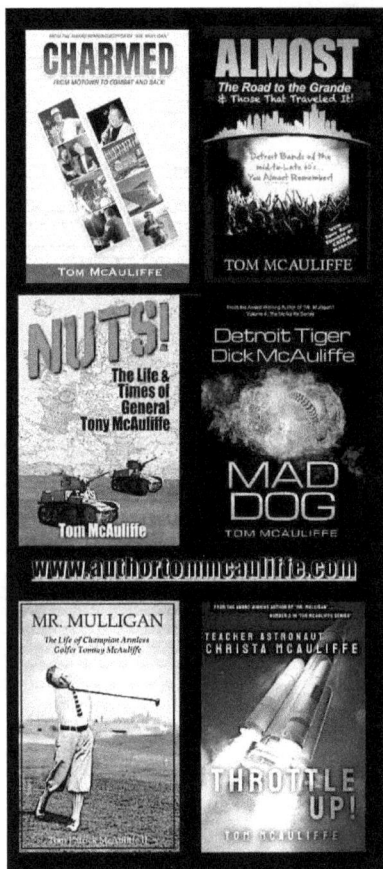

- Mr. Mulligan - *The Life of Champion Armless Golfer Tommy McAuliffe*

- NUTS! - *The Life & Times of General Tony McAuliffe*

- Throttle Up - *Teacher Astronaut Christa McAuliffe*

- Mad Dog - *Detroit Tiger Dick McAuliffe*

- Charmed - *From Motown to Combat & Back*

- Almost - *The Road to the Grande*

Available everywhere as
Books, eBooks and Audiobooks!

www.ingramcontent.com/pod-product-compliance
Lightning Source LLC
Chambersburg PA
CBHW060924040426
42445CB00011B/777